Making Sense of It All

"Pastor Hipps is a man acquainted with grief, and also with joy. All the stories he tells, by way of illustrating matters of faith, show God's grace at work in human hearts. I can't think of anything more the world needs today than stories like these which refract the light of God's good story into our daily lives."

—**Susan S. Phillips**, author of *The Cultivated Life: From Ceaseless Striving to Receiving Joy*

"Forged in the depths of doubt and despair, *Making Sense of It All* is rooted in Richard Hipps' core Christian belief that 'a good God is telling a good story that will have a good ending.' Don't be surprised if you experience a surge of hope, gratitude, and joy reading this book, especially if you've been feeling bereft, beleaguered, or confused."

—**Lee Kravitz**, author of *Unfinished Business: One Man's Extraordinary Year of Trying to Do the Right Things*

"Writing with the accumulated wisdom of decades of fruitful ministry, Richard Hipps offers readers a rich feast of pastoral and theological wisdom. Throughout this book, in every chapter, every page, deep calls to deep, offering readers both comfort and hope. *Making Sense of It All* is the book you should press into the hands of people facing heartaches and trials. They will thank you."

—**Cheryl Bridges Johns**, director, Pentecostal House of Study, United Theological Seminary

"These pages come from a pastor's heart that repeatedly affirms that 'a good God is telling a good story that will have a good ending.' The whole book might be summarized with this one sentence: 'The worst thing that ever happens to you will not be the final thing. Love will have the final move.' If you finish the book convinced of this . . . well, only God knows what might happen then."

—**DAVID C. STANCIL**, retired pastor and professor

"In this book, Richard Hipps shares a story of his encounter with John Wimber. Like most useful stories, it chronicles a conversion of thinking. An 'aha' moment. An epiphany. I would like to hear more epiphanies from the pulpit. Most of us hope that our pastors grow with time, but we rarely learn the intimate details of that metamorphosis that might help them seem more human to us. Richard shares those details."

—**DIANE KOMP**, professor emeritus of pediatrics, Yale University School of Medicine

Making Sense of It All

A Pastor's Best Guesses about God's Good Story

Richard S. Hipps

RESOURCE *Publications* · Eugene, Oregon

MAKING SENSE OF IT ALL
A Pastor's Best Guesses about God's Good Story

Copyright © 2024 Richard S. Hipps. All rights reserved. Except for brief quotations in critical publications or reviews, no part of this book may be reproduced in any manner without prior written permission from the publisher. Write: Permissions, Wipf and Stock Publishers, 199 W. 8th Ave., Suite 3, Eugene, OR 97401.

Resource Publications
An Imprint of Wipf and Stock Publishers
199 W. 8th Ave., Suite 3
Eugene, OR 97401

www.wipfandstock.com

PAPERBACK ISBN: 978-1-6667-8721-4
HARDCOVER ISBN: 978-1-6667-8722-1
EBOOK ISBN: 978-1-6667-8723-8

VERSION NUMBER 02/14/24

All Scripture references are from The Holy Bible, Today's New International Version TNIV Copyright © 2001, 2005 by The Zondervan Corporation unless otherwise noted.

With love and gratitude to my Patricia—
faithful wife, wise counselor, and incessant encourager.

For our grandchildren—
Braden, Isla, Ezra, Alexandra, and Beau

When we submit our lives to what we read in scripture, we find that we are not being led to see God in our stories but our stories in God's. God is the larger context and plot in which our stories find themselves.

—Eugene Peterson

Contents

Introduction | ix

1. Relinquish | 1
2. Election | 9
3. Guest | 18
4. Surrender | 24
5. Children | 33
6. Peacemaking | 41
7. Doubt | 49
8. Miracles | 57
9. Discouragement | 66
10. Unique | 76
11. Grace | 83
12. Metanarrative | 92
13. Galilee | 100
14. Trust | 106
15. Angels | 117
16. Forgiveness | 126
17. Hope | 135

Bibliography | 145

Introduction

I ONCE HEARD A seminary professor say, "Be careful how you use the phrase '*the Bible says.*'" Instead, people should say, "*From my understanding*, this is what the Bible says." Why is that? Because all of us interpret what we see and experience, including what we see and experience when reading the Bible. In fact, all reading is interpretation, and what is being read must work itself through several layers of filters. We may have rarely even considered these filters.

Take *age* for instance. I do not read and understand scripture at the age of seventy the same way I did when I was in my twenties (and I have sermons to prove it). Decades of life experience and study have changed the way I interpret what I read.

My *race* affects the way I interpret scripture. Prior to the Civil War many sermons were preached in favor of slavery by white clergy. Can you imagine an African American preacher delivering the same message? Even today, you can be sure blacks and whites read and emotionally interpret scripture like Ephesians 6:5 very differently:

> Slaves, obey your earthly masters with respect and fear, and with sincerity of heart, just as you would obey Christ.

And then there is *culture*, a large part of which is nationality. I learned this the hard way as a missionary in Brazil. Along with the gospel, I carried a lot of invisible baggage with me to South America. My Brazilian students and colleagues were quick to point out my Americanized form of Christianity. We all have cultural assumptions that influence the way we interpret the Bible.

Introduction

You can add these additional filters to those mentioned above: *current perspective on world history, personal history, intelligence, education, imagination, desires, prejudices, giftedness, and physical health* as well as any number of other factors. They all influence the way we understand and interpret God's Word.

Humility is needed when we come to interpret the Bible. I am realizing more and more how arrogant I was in my younger days. I assumed that the most correct understanding of the Bible was my way of understanding the Bible. However, only God sees things as they truly are—and I am not God. Neither is Augustine, Luther, Billy Graham, the pope, or you. We all "see through a glass darkly" as Eugene Peterson's *The Message* beautifully paraphrases 1 Corinthians 13:12:

> We don't yet see things clearly. We're squinting in a fog, peering through a mist. But it won't be long before the weather clears and the sun shines bright! We'll see it all then, see it all as clearly as God sees us, knowing him directly just as he knows us!

Don't get me wrong. I believe we can know the truth, but I do not think we can be absolutely sure that what we believe is, in fact, the whole truth and nothing but the truth.

At a funeral years ago, the preacher said that the deceased was probably in hell. I could not believe what I was hearing. I thought, *You do not know that. How dare you even suggest such a thing! That is God's decision and God's decision alone.* It is God who says, "I will have mercy on whom I will have mercy, and I will have compassion on whom I will have compassion" (Exodus 33:19). We judge from outward appearances, but God looks on the heart. Only God sees things as they are. With God's help, we can see things truly, but never wholly.

The most brilliant theologian who ever lived cannot know all there is to know about God and God's ways. We are always going to come up short unless we are guided and inspired by the Holy Spirit. Humbling ourselves is what God requires.

In his book *The Power of a Humble Life: Quiet Strength in an Age of Arrogance*, Richard E. Simmons III writes,

Introduction

> Grace is a word that is often misunderstood and literally means receiving God's favor. The most common definition used in the Bible is the unmerited favor of God, which applies to salvation. But in the New Testament, the word grace is most commonly applied to living this life with God's power—a divine enablement. Through grace, God enables us to do that which we cannot do ourselves (Hebrews 13:9, 2 Timothy 2:1). Grace is incredibly significant. God gives his strength and power only to the humble through grace.[1]

A divine enablement given to the humble reader will render the best and most accurate interpretation of God's Word.

In this book, I am simply offering my best guesses at understanding life with God that make sense to me. Take what helps you and forget what does not. My aim is not to provoke arguments but to get you to think more deeply about your own faith journey. I do so with humility, kindness, and the understanding that my knowledge is incomplete. Even though my knowledge is limited, I have a great desire to share my own journey. I am not implying that my experience should be your experience, but the more we share, the more we grow in our understanding of just how big and wonderful the story of Jesus is.

The chapters in this book are snapshots of my basic beliefs, and you will find one belief in particular that runs throughout the book: *a good God is telling a good story that will have a good ending*. As Lewis B. Smedes said in his spiritual memoir, *My Hope Goes for Broke*,

> C. S Lewis said somewhere that when God comes back to earth it will be like having the author of a play on stage after the final performance; the play is over, he takes his bow, the players leave and the theater is swallowed in darkness. I do not much like his metaphor. I believe that the Author of the play will appear on stage not after the final performance, but before the curtain rises. The players have been turning rehearsals into nasty fights about who gets the best lines and the prime spot on the

---

1. Simmons, *The Power of a Humble Life*, 55.

Introduction

billboard; the play has become a disaster, doomed before it gets off the ground. It is then that the Author shows up, his original script in hand and with the power to change self-seeking egos into self-giving artists. The theater is bathed in gentle light, the curtain rises, and the play begins a triumphant endless run. Not the ending, but the new beginning—this is what I hope for.[2]

My suggestion to you, dear reader, is to simply read what I have written with an open mind and an open heart and see where it leads. Together, let us learn everything we can about God and his world. Let's prioritize trust in Jesus and give him our heads and our hearts.

---

2. Smedes, *My Hope Goes for Broke*, 172.

1

Relinquish

Jesus went out as usual to the Mount of Olives, and his disciples followed him. On reaching the place, he said to them, "Pray that you will not fall into temptation." He withdrew about a stone's throw beyond them, knelt down and prayed, "Father, if you are willing, take this cup from me; yet not my will, but yours be done." An angel from heaven appeared to him and strengthened him.

—Luke 22:39–43

When you remember me, it means you have carried something of who I am with you, that I have left some mark of who I am on who you are. It means you can summon me back to your mind even though countless years and miles may stand between us. It means that if we meet again, you will know me. It means that even after I die, you can still see my face and hear my voice and speak to me in your heart.

—Frederick Buechner

Relinquish

I WILL NEVER FORGET February 14, 1993. It was a Sunday, Valentine's Day, and we were Brazilian missionaries on furlough and living in Smyrna, Georgia. A church had kindly offered its missionary residence for the year we would be in the United States.

At five o'clock on Sunday morning, our phone rang, and it was the pastor of our host church. He had been up most of the night with a stomach virus and was unable to preach that morning. "Can you step in for me?" he asked.

"Of course," I said. "I am happy to do so."

Hanging up the phone, I prayerfully began to think about what God would have me say to the congregation that morning. Having only a few hours to prepare, I anxiously remembered that the church's services were televised.

That very week, I had been thinking about a story I had heard about a missionary who was retiring after serving for nearly four decades in the field. He had returned to his home church—the one that had commissioned him all those years earlier—and told the churchgoers a story that touched me deeply.

As a young man leaving for language study, he decided to spend some time in prayer in his home church's sanctuary when no one was present. He took with him a list of promises he was offering to the Lord as a newly commissioned missionary. It was a long list, and he had signed his name at the bottom of the page.

After about an hour of praying his promises, he got up and left the altar. On his way to his car, he felt a tugging at his heart, and he whispered, "Lord, what is it? For some reason, I don't feel at peace about our time together." With that, he put his keys back into his pocket and returned to the sanctuary.

After sitting quietly for several minutes, he heard within himself the voice of the Lord: "Turn your page of promises over, sign your name at the bottom, and leave the paper blank. I will fill it in as I choose." The missionary, in faith, did just that, and it made all the difference in the world.

I used this story in my sermon that morning to tell the congregation that the missionary had said his signing a blank page of paper was the greatest decision he had ever made. In doing so, he was choosing God's plan and God's agenda and leaving his own agenda behind.

I then asked the congregation if each of them would be willing to do the same: sign their names on a blank sheet of paper and allow God to fill it in as he chose with good times and bad, happy and sad, days of sickness and days of health, days of poverty and days of wealth.

Holding up my own newly signed blank sheet of paper, I asked them to commit to doing the same. I was moved to see so many respond. They came to the front, took the blank sheet of paper I had provided, and returned to their pews. Little did I know that God was preparing me for the darkest day of my life.

Exactly two Sundays later, on February 28, 1993, we were in Green Hills Cemetery in Asheville, North Carolina, burying our youngest child, Leigh Alexandra. She was just two months shy of her fifth birthday. Myocarditis, an inflammation of the heart muscle, took her from us suddenly and without warning.

The last photo that we have of our family together was snapped by a church member two weeks earlier, the morning I had asked everyone to sign a blank sheet of paper allowing God to write his or her story, good times and bad, happy or sad, days of sickness and days of health, days of poverty and days of wealth.

In my life and ministry, Alex's death has caused me to focus on the will of God more than any other event in my life. How does the death of one's child shape one's understanding of God, especially when it comes to understanding one's child's death in the context of God's will, God's script, and God's plan?

I have never understood the thinking of those who say their child's death was in no way God's will. I have never doubted that God is deeply moved by our grief and truly cares about our suffering because he loves us. But to imply that our child's death is not part of a plan beyond our comprehension would make my suffering even worse.

A couple of years after Alex's death, I edited a book called *When a Child Dies: Stories of Survival and Hope*. Along with my own story, nine others shared the stories of their children's

Relinquish

deaths and how they survived the unimaginable. It was our hope that grieving families would find strength for their own difficult journeys.

The original title for my book was not *When a Child Dies* but *Little Ones to Him Belong*, which was taken from the song *Jesus Loves Me*.

> Jesus loves me! this I know,
> For the Bible tells me so;
> Little ones to him belong;
> They are weak, but he is strong.

The editors rejected my original title, saying it would imply that God had something to do with our children's deaths. I argued against the change, but the editors were adamant.

Anyone who buries a child must come to terms with it theologically. I could not sleep at night if my child's death was not in some way meaningful to God's larger story. When I signed that blank sheet of paper on February 14, 1993, I committed to believing that since God is good, his plan is good, and the great cosmic story he is weaving will indeed have a good ending. A good God would do no less than bring something good from my child's death, something I will understand fully when I no longer see through a glass darkly.

Please don't *over-hear* what I am saying. Even though I do believe that all events fall within God's good story, I do not believe that every single event is, in isolation, a good thing. For this reason, I know that I will never understand Alexandra's death, in isolation, this side of heaven.

I have chosen to take the long view placing my hope in the resurrection of Jesus Christ. Because Jesus lives, I know that a new creation is coming and that everything wrong will be made right, including the death of my little child.

I am committed and fully submitted to the absolute sovereignty of God and affirm with the apostle Paul that our suffering is temporary, but the gain is eternal:

Relinquish

> For our light and momentary troubles are achieving for us an eternal glory that far outweighs them all (2 Corinthians 4:17).

Joy and sorrow can be friends, as Stephen Shortridge beautifully argues:

> Up until now I couldn't have imagined that joy and sorrow could be friends and not enemies. In God's economy joy and sorrow might be like two sides of the same coin, not unlike faith and works. In some ways, the depths of sorrow measure the heights of joy. If I embrace the tragedy of this life, ironically, I also experience greater joy the larger and greater the space that is created between. Not a vacuum, but a positive space that is created between. Not a vacuum but a positive space that God will fill with his love.[1]

Isn't that exactly what scripture tells us about Jesus?

> And let us run with perseverance the race marked out for us, fixing our eyes on Jesus, the pioneer and perfecter of faith. For the joy set before him he endured the cross, scorning its shame, and sat down at the right hand of the throne of God. Consider him who endured such opposition from sinners, so that you will not grow weary and lose heart (Hebrews 12:1–3).

I love the way Eugene Peterson's *The Message* paraphrases those same verses.

> Keep your eyes on Jesus, who both began and finished this race we're in. Study how he did it. Because he never lost sight of where he was and where he was headed—that exhilarating finish in and with God—he could put up with anything along the way: Cross, shame, whatever. And now he's *there,* in the place of honor, right alongside God. When you find yourselves flagging in your faith, go over that story again, item by item, that long litany of hostility he plowed through. *That* will shoot adrenaline into your souls!

---

1. Shortridge, *Deepest Thanks, Deeper Apologies*, 79–80.

Relinquish

Charles Spurgeon, that great Baptist preacher of the nineteenth century, said, "It is not a curious thing that, whenever God means to make a man great, he always breaks him in pieces first."

> Have none of you ever noticed, in your own lives, that whenever God is going to give you an enlargement, and bring you out to a larger sphere of service, or a higher platform of spiritual life, you always get thrown down? That is his usual way of working; he makes you hungry before he feeds you; he strips you before he robes you; he makes nothing of you before he makes something of you. This was the way with David. He is to be king in Jerusalem; but he must go to the throne by way of the cave. Now are any of you here going to heaven, or going to a more heavenly state of sanctification, or going to a greater sphere of usefulness: Do not wonder if you go by way of the cave.[2]

The deepest desire of our Lord Jesus was to always be in the center of his Father's will. He wanted more than anything to do those things that would establish the kingdom of God—even if it meant the Cross of Calvary:

> Father, if you are willing, take this cup from me; yet not my will, but yours be done (Luke 22:42).

When the unbearable, unthinkable, unimaginable invade our lives, and they will, we must carefully choose the proper response. And, let me say, not choosing is also a response, albeit a poor one.

A woman named JoAnne Lyon tells of her resentment against God because of her inability for many years to bear children. Confessing this, she saw she only had two choices—relinquish or resign:

> I could either relinquish my infertility or resign myself to it. The difference between the two is subtle but powerful. I picture it this way: to relinquish a circumstance is to approach God with an open hand, saying, "Here it is, Lord. I don't know what to do with this, but I look forward to what you'll do." Relinquishment is not an attempt to second-guess God or to manipulate him. It is an act of

---

2. Spurgeon, *The Treasury of the Old Testament*, 155.

Relinquish

willing surrender. To resign, on the other hand, is to approach God with a closed hand—a fist—saying, "If this is the way life has to be, then I'll grit my teeth and bear it, I'll accept this thing, but nothing on earth will ever make me like it." Resignation accepts the circumstance but stubbornly resists God in the process.[3]

We spend way too much of our lives trying to make sense of everything that happens. One giant leap in our faith journey is when we accept the fact that some things do not make sense. Some questions will not have answers.

Gilda Radner, the comedienne who died in 1989 from cancer, said, "Some poems don't rhyme, and some stories don't have a clear beginning, middle, and end."[4] That being the case, I plan to spend the rest of my days relinquishing those unanswered questions to a good God who is writing a good story that will have a good ending. Trusting God has become more important to me than understanding God.

When we choose God's agenda over our own, we soon learn that it can involve pain, suffering, and sometimes *angels*. Heaven will send those special people to help us not give up and continue on our journey of faith:

> He withdrew about a stone's throw beyond them, knelt down and prayed, "Father, if you are willing, take this cup from me; yet not my will, but yours be done. An angel from heaven appeared to him and strengthened him" (Luke 22:41–43).

An angel came and strengthened me also about a month after Alex died. In the most vivid dream I have ever had, perhaps more than a dream, an older woman came to me holding my little daughter's hand. Alex looked so radiant, so healthy, and so happy. I fell to my knees, weeping, and said, "Oh, God, it was only a terrible dream. Alex didn't die. Thank you, God. Thank you, God."

---

3. Simon, *Rediscovering the Lord's Prayer*, 60.
4. Radner, *It's Always Something*, 268.

Relinquish

The woman, who I seemed to know but didn't recognize, placed her hand on my shoulder and gently said, "Richard, you know she can't stay, but we will take good care of her until you get home."

Amazingly, I said, "OK."

With that, Alex and her guardian walked away and my little daughter turned around and blew me a kiss as she often did.

Stories such as mine are seldom heard because we are afraid of what others might think. These days, there seems to be an aversion to all things supernatural. We have diluted our vision of heaven and lost interest in God's invisible kingdom. We resist any notion of a heavenly existence and are emphatic in finding our fulfillment in this life and no other.

I can assure you that I am not in denial or stuck in one of the many stages of grief. It will soon be thirty years since Alex left us. I simply long for more than this world has to offer. The joy that is set before me, the hope of heaven, helps me endure. It keeps me going. I relinquished my child into the hands of the Good Shepherd all those years ago, and I am sure the lady in my dream and so many others are enjoying her company and taking good care of her as promised. More importantly, she is with Jesus—and that is what matters most. What God creates, he loves, and what God loves, he loves forever. We either believe that—or we do not.

Christopher Columbus died in 1506 in the Spanish city of Valladolid. In the city, a monument commemorates the great explorer. An interesting feature of the memorial is the statue of a lion at the base where the Spanish National Motto is engraved. The lion is extending its paw and destroying one of the Latin words that had been part of Spain's motto for centuries. Before Columbus made his famous voyages, the Spaniards thought they had reached the ends of the earth—thus their motto was *No More Beyond*. The word being ripped away by the lion is *No*, making it now read *More Beyond*. Columbus had proven there was indeed more beyond. The same is true for those chosen by Jesus. There is more beyond.

2

Election

Isaac prayed to the Lord on behalf of his wife, because she was childless. The Lord answered his prayer, and his wife Rebekah became pregnant. The babies jostled each other within her, and she said, "Why is this happening to me?" So she went to inquire of the Lord. The Lord said to her,

"Two nations are in your womb,
and two peoples from within you will be separated;
one people will be stronger than the other,
and the older will serve the younger."

When the time came for her to give birth, there were twin boys in her womb. The first to come out was red, and his whole body was like a hairy garment; so they named him Esau. After this, his brother came out, with his hand grasping Esau's heel; so he was named Jacob. Isaac was sixty years old when Rebekah gave birth to them.

—Genesis 25:21–26

Election

> I believe in the doctrine of election, because I am quite sure that if God had not chosen me I should never have chosen him; and I am sure he chose me before I was born, or else he never would have chosen me afterwards; and he must have elected me for reasons unknown to me, for I never could find any reason in myself why.
>
> —CHARLES SPURGEON

I HAVE ALWAYS BEEN interested in asking people to tell me their favorite Bible character because I believe we are predisposed to be drawn to a particular person or story. That is why I also encourage others to study the Bible biographically.

One advantage to reading the Bible biographically is that our brains remember stories much better than trivia or arbitrary facts. Studying scripture biographically gives flesh to biblical truth. It is truth clothed in human personality.

Another thing we discover in reading the Bible biographically is that the Bible never sugarcoats the truth, not even with its heroes. Nothing is censored, hidden, or excused. It is the truth, the whole truth, and nothing but the truth.

This is seen clearly in the life of Jacob. He has the same weaknesses, longings, ambiguities, and neediness that each of us does. As R. Paul Stevens suggests,

> Jacob's story is so universal because it is so personal. He grows up with an emotionally distant father and bonds deeply with his mother. The family is fragmented and messy. While his parent's marriage began in love, his mother and father grew emotionally distant from each other, and each parent sought intimacy and solace in a favorite child. A distant father, an overbearing mother, an overpowering brother, wives he cannot please, a manipulative father-in-law, children alienated from each

Election

other—this is the stuff not only of Jacob's story, but all too often of our own.[1]

The story of Jacob runs counter to the thinking of our world. Most religions propose that good people are in and bad people are out, but that is clearly not the case in the life of Jacob. The rock group U2 could easily be singing about Jacob in their song *Grace*. In one line, Bono, the lead singer and writer of the lyrics, sings, "Grace travels outside of karma." In a recent interview, he explained what he meant:

> It's a mind-blowing concept that the God who created the universe might be looking for company, a real relationship with people, but the thing that keeps me on my knees is the difference between grace and karma.
>
> You see, at the center of all religions is the idea of karma. You know, what you put out comes back to you—an eye for an eye, a tooth for a tooth, or any physics in physical laws—every action is met by an equal or opposite one. It's clear to me that karma is at the very heart of the universe. I'm absolutely sure of it.
>
> And yet, along comes this idea called grace to up end all that "as you sow, so shall you reap" stuff. Grace defies reason and logic. Love interrupts, if you like, the consequences of your actions, which in my case is very good news indeed, because I've done a lot of stupid stuff.
>
> That's between me and God. But I'd be in big trouble if karma was going to finally be my judge . . . It doesn't excuse my mistakes, but I'm holding out for grace. I'm holding out that Jesus took my sins onto the cross because I know who I am, and I hope I don't have to depend on my own religiosity.[2]

I am sure Jacob would agree. Our relationship with God is not based on anything we have done or not done. It is the work of God from beginning to end. It is unmerited, unconditional, irresistible, and inexplicable.

What did God say to Rebekah in response to her prayer?

1. Stevens, *Down-to-Earth Spirituality*, 15.
2. Assayas, *Bono in Conversation with Michka Assayas*, 203–4.

Election

> Two nations are in your womb, and two peoples from within you will be separated; one people will be stronger than the other, and the older will serve the younger (Genesis 25:23).

Before the twins are born, there is a differentiation. One would be heir to the promise, and one would not. The apostle Paul confirms this differentiation:

> Not only that, but Rebekah's children were conceived at the same time by our father Isaac. Yet, before the twins were born or had done anything good or bad—in order that God's purpose in election might stand: not by works but by him who calls—she was told, "The older will serve the younger" (Romans 9:10–12).

The war in Rebekah's womb had nothing to do with her or Isaac. It was God and God alone working out his plan and purpose through their lives. In the words of Griffith Thomas, "The order of nature is not necessarily the order of grace."[3]

> For he chose us in him before the creation of the world to be holy and blameless in his sight. In love he predestined us for adoption to sonship through Jesus Christ, in accordance with his pleasure and will—to the praise of his glorious grace, which he has freely given us in the One he loves. In him we have redemption through his blood, the forgiveness of sins, in accordance with the riches of God's grace that he lavished on us. (Ephesians 1:4–8).

In his testimony to the Galatians, the apostle Paul confirmed his own election:

> But when God, who set me apart from birth and called me by his grace, was pleased to reveal his Son in me so that I might preach him among the Gentiles, my immediate response was not to consult any human being. I did not go up to Jerusalem to see those who were apostles before I was, but I went into Arabia. Later I returned to Damascus (Galatians 1:15–17).

---

3. Thomas, *Genesis*, 252.

Notice how Paul does not say, "When I decided to follow Jesus" or "When I asked Jesus to come into my heart." Nobody in the Bible talks like that.

A man in China giving his testimony in a church meeting was asked, "How did you come to know the Lord?" The man spoke modestly about how God had sought him, opened his heart to receive the truth, and how the Holy Spirit had given him a new birth and made of him a new creation.

As he finished, someone said, "That's a wonderful testimony, but you didn't tell us anything you did to become a Christian."

The man responded, "I don't know what you mean. There's nothing I did."

The person persisted, asking, "We understand God did his part, but you must have done something. What was your part?"

Half smiling, the Chinese convert said, "Oh, yes, my part! I ran and ran as far from God as I could. I tried to get away from him, but his part was to run faster, tackle me, and totally overcome me with his love."

Election, being chosen, means God all by himself saves sinners.

Herschel Hobbs, a giant among Southern Baptists in the twentieth century, wrote a sermon called *God's Election Day*. Here is a summary of his main point:

> The devil and God held an election to determine whether or not you would be saved or lost. The devil voted against you and God voted for you. So the vote was a tie . . . It's up to you to cast the deciding vote.[4]

Sounds reasonable, but is it biblical?

> Among Protestants there are three main views regarding the doctrine of election and all three appear in scripture. Naturally all three claim the other two fall short of biblical and theological correctness, but all three affirm divine initiative—it is God who acts.[5]

---

4. Olson, "Election Is for Everyone," 42.
5. Olson, "Election Is for Everyone," 42.

Election

The first view is classical Calvinism. This line of thinking came to be associated with Calvin, but Luther and Zwingli held similar views about election. God is sovereign in all things, including every person's eternal destiny. God in his sovereignty has elected some to eternal life and some to eternal damnation.

The second view is classical Arminianism. This view derives its name from the theologian Arminius, but the basic ideas predate him. The most influential Arminian would no doubt be John Wesley, the founder of Methodism. According to Wesley, God foreknew those in every nation who would eventually believe, and God elected them from the beginning of the world to the end.[6]

Most contemporary evangelical Christians either lean toward Wesley or Calvin about election, but they divide over individual salvation, especially about whether God predestines some people to hell. Arminians like Wesley find it unacceptable and damaging to God's reputation to suggest he would predestine some to hell:

> For God so loved the world that he gave his one and only Son, that whoever believes in him shall not perish but have eternal life (John 3:16).

> The Lord is not slow in keeping his promise, as some understand slowness. Instead he is patient with you, not wanting anyone to perish, but everyone to come to repentance (2 Peter 3:9).

> This is good, and pleases God our Savior, who wants all people to be saved and to come to a knowledge of the truth (1 Timothy 2:3–4).

Calvinists counter with verses like:

> You did not choose me, but I chose you and appointed you so that you might go and bear fruit—fruit that will last (John 15:16).

> When the Gentiles heard this, they were glad and honored the word of the Lord; and all who were appointed for eternal life believed (Acts 13:48).

---

6. Olson, "Election Is for Everyone," 42.

Election

> For certain individuals whose condemnation was written about long ago have secretly slipped in among you. They are ungodly people, who pervert the grace of our God into a license for immorality and deny Jesus Christ our only Sovereign and Lord (Jude 1:4).

We can see how each group uses scripture to bolster its theological position.[7]

The third view was influenced by pastor/theologian Karl Barth. Barth is considered by many to be the most influential theologian since the Reformation. Barth's understanding of election begins and ends with Christ. Christ is the elected one in whom all humanity is elected. Christ is also the one who is rejected and dies on our behalf. Jesus Christ is the elected man *and* the electing God. He, as God, elects himself as man in Christ, and we are included in his humanity.

This way of understanding election gives Paul's words a whole new and deeper meaning:

> Consequently, just as one trespass resulted in condemnation for all people, so also one righteous act resulted in justification and life for all. For just as through the disobedience of one man the many were made sinners, so also through the obedience of the one man the many will be made righteous (Romans 5:18–19).

> For God has bound everyone over to disobedience so that he may have mercy on them all (Romans 11:32).

> For as in Adam all die, so in Christ all will be made alive (I Corinthians 15:22).

In this third view, all are included in Christ's salvific work, thereby making salvation by grace alone and Christ alone. Being elected in Christ is good news because it is not dependent on the frail and faltering free will of sinners, which leads some to assume Barth and his followers are universalists. Barth, however, did not fully

---

7. Olson, "Election Is for Everyone," 42.

Election

embrace universalism because he believed no one can know with certainty what a sovereign God will do.[8]

Biblically, it is impossible to ignore the doctrine of election and almost as impossible to understand it. Scripture is quite clear in that there was absolutely no merit or goodness that caused God to choose us. As hard as it is to comprehend, the Bible teaches both election and free will.

Charles Spurgeon, the great Baptist preacher, was asked to reconcile election and free will, God's sovereignty and man's responsibility, and he said, "I never try to reconcile friends—they are both in the Bible."

> Whatever may be said about the doctrine of election, it is written in the word of God as with an iron pen, and there is no getting rid of it. To me, it is one of the sweetest and most blessed truths in the whole of revelation, and those who are afraid of it are so because they don't understand it. If they could but know that the Lord has chosen them, it would make their hearts dance for joy.[9]

Throughout scripture, as with Jacob, we see so many examples of God choosing people who are not used to being chosen. And what is true for Jacob is true for us all—as the apostle Paul wrote in his first letter to the Corinthians:

> Brothers and sisters, think of what you were when you were called. Not many of you were wise by human standards; not many were influential; not many were of noble birth. But God chose the foolish things of the world to shame the wise; God chose the weak things of the world to shame the strong. God chose the lowly things of this world and the despised things—and the things that are not—to nullify the things that are, so that no one may boast before him (1 Corinthians 1:26–29).

These grace-filled words motivate us to want to make good choices ourselves. However, our choices—right and wrong—will

---

8. Olson, "Election Is for Everyone," 42.
9. Spurgeon, *Spurgeon's Sermons*, 375.

Election

not determine the sum of our lives—not by a long shot. Someone else's choice will determine that. The sum of our life is not the choices we make, but the choice Jesus made. It will be his faithfulness, not ours, that meets us on the other side of life.

3

Guest

Early in the morning, Jesus stood on the shore, but the disciples did not realize that it was Jesus. He called out to them, "Friends, haven't you any fish?" "No," they answered. He said, "Throw your net on the right side of the boat and you will find some." When they did, they were unable to haul the net in because of the large number of fish. Then the disciple whom Jesus loved said to Peter, "It is the Lord!" As soon as Simon Peter heard him say, "It is the Lord," he wrapped his outer garment around him (for he had taken it off) and jumped into the water. The other disciples followed in the boat, towing the net full of fish, for they were not far from the shore, about a hundred yards. When they landed, they saw a fire of burning coals there with fish on it, and some bread. Jesus said to them, "Bring some of the fish you have just caught." Simon Peter climbed aboard and dragged the net ashore. It was full of large fish, 153, but even with so many the net was not torn. Jesus said, "Come and have breakfast."

—JOHN 21:4–12

Guest

> Do you believe that the God of Jesus loves you beyond worthiness and unworthiness, beyond fidelity and infidelity—that he loves you in the morning sun and in the evening rain—that he loves you when your intellect denies it, your emotions refuse it, your whole being rejects it? Do you believe that God loves without condition or reservation and loves you this moment as you are and not as you should be?
>
> —BRENNAN MANNING

I LOVE ENTERING CRACKER Barrel early in the morning with the smell of bacon and coffee greeting me at the door. Breakfast has always been my favorite meal. Perhaps that is why the story of Jesus cooking breakfast for his disciples over a charcoal fire by the Sea of Galilee is one of my favorite Bible stories. Of all the things you would expect Jesus to say to his followers after he rose from the dead, especially since all of them betrayed and abandoned him, would not be "Come and have breakfast. Be my guest."

Have you given much thought to what it means to be God's guest? We are so accustomed to seeing ourselves in the role of host that it is hard to assume the role of guest. We even assume the role of host when we invite God into our hearts when, in fact, it is God who invites us into his.

God is host, we are guests, and the image of guest says almost nothing about our responsibilities. Its emphasis falls entirely on our privileges. We simply show up and enjoy God's hospitality. As Joseph Joubert says, "To be an agreeable guest, one need only to enjoy oneself."[1]

Why is it so hard for us to view God as gracious host? When some people think about God, they start with a negative image. They picture God as a God who quickly punishes people when they do wrong—a God who is a stern judge, sitting behind his bench with gavel in hand, always ready to pronounce people guilty.

---

1. Joubert, *A Selection from His Thoughts*, 61

Guest

We know God hates sin because the cross is central to our faith, but let us rejoice in the fact that God's desire to have us with him is of higher priority than his desire to punish us. In order to deal with our sin, our rejection of God's hospitality, Jesus, our Lord, offered up his own life, absorbing our rebellion, enabling us once again to be guests at God's table, permanent members of God's family. It is very good news indeed that God, our generous host, will not allow the rejection of his hospitality to be the last word.

Our concept of God determines the kind of people we become. If we serve an angry God, we will be angry people. If our God keeps a ledger of wrongs, we will keep a ledger of wrongs. If our God accepts us when we are good and rejects us when we are bad, then we will accept people when they are good and reject them when they are bad. We will treat others the way we think God treats us.

Because of Jesus Christ, we should believe that God is madly in love with us. And yet, sadly, so few of us believe this. It is so hard for us to believe that we are accepted as we are, forgiven for all our sins—past, present, and future—and continually cared for by a loving and gracious Savior.

The gospel truth is that God's love and mercy are the only things that can radically reshape our identity. Julian of Norwich wrote, "The greatest honor that we can give to Almighty God is to live gladly because of the knowledge of his love."[2]

In 1 Corinthians 13:4–8, we are given a beautiful description of God's love toward us:

> Love is patient, love is kind. It does not envy, it does not boast, it is not proud. It does not dishonor others, it is not self-seeking, it is not easily angered, it keeps no record of wrongs. Love does not delight in evil but rejoices with the truth. It always protects, always trusts, always hopes, always perseveres. Love never fails.

As incredible as it sounds, this is exactly how God loves every one of us. He is patient with us. He understands our faults and failures. He is kind to us. He gives us what we need and not what we

---

2. Manning, *The Ragamuffin Gospel*, 34.

deserve. He is not boastful. Why would he need to boast? He is not rude. He has no need to offend or insult us. He keeps no records of our wrongs. We don't have to fear a future condemnation.

God lives by the same standard of love that he asks us to live by. He tells us not to track the wrongs that others do to us. He tells us not to punish those who harm us. He tells us not to harbor grudges and to forgive seventy times seven. He tells us to pray for our enemies and to love those who spitefully use us.

If God keeps a ledger of our wrongs, then he is not as loving as he demands us to be. If God doesn't forgive seventy times seven, why does he command us to do so? For some, God is more accountant than he is lover.

When we finally meet God, how will he receive us? Will he check his little list like Santa to see if we have been naughty or nice? Will he give us a grade? I have often imagined meeting my grandmother and mother and little daughter someday on that blessed shore and the love we will feel in that sweet reunion. But imagine meeting God who is pure omnipotent, omniscient, omnipresent love.

Many mistakenly believe that upon his return to heaven, the Son of God shed his humanity and returned to his previous existence as simply God. Some think the Son, the second member of the Trinity, is no longer Jesus, that he is no longer human, or at least he will not be human forever. Scripture teaches something altogether different. The union of the divine and human in Jesus is an eternal reality. The Logos gave up his unique and exclusive existence as God to also become human, to add humanity to himself, and human he will remain. His humanity is now as much a part of his identity as his divinity.

Jesus did not cease to be God to become human, but he also did not put on humanity as a temporary cloak. Wounded, fallen, sin-sick humanity needs to learn to what lengths God has gone to get us home. Scripture affirms this:

> Who, being in very nature God, did not consider equality with God something to be used to his own advantage; rather he made himself nothing by taking the very nature

of a servant, being made in human likeness. And being found in appearance as a human being, he humbled himself by becoming obedient to death—even death on a cross! Therefore God exalted him to the highest place and gave him the name that is above every name, that at the name of Jesus every knee should bow, in heaven and on earth and under the earth, and every tongue acknowledge that Jesus Christ is Lord, to the glory of God the Father (Philippians 2:6–11).

Will Willimon described Carlyle Marney's visit to Wofford College as the guest preacher for religious emphasis week. Dr. Marney, a prominent Baptist minister, was a mentor and role model to pastors of every denomination. A group of students had the opportunity to sit and talk with Marney about their individual callings and shared ministry:

> During their discussion one student asked, "Dr. Marney, let us hear you say a word or two about the resurrection from the dead." It was a fair question, but the students were not prepared for Marney's answer. "I will not discuss that with people like you." "Why not?" they asked. Marney responded, "Look at you! Just look at you. You are in the prime of your life, full of talent and energy. Very few if any of you have experienced poverty, failure, defeat, heartbreak or a brick wall that stops you dead in your tracks. So, tell me, what in God's name can any of you know of a dark harsh world which only makes sense if Christ is raised from the dead?"[3]

Unlike these students, the apostle Peter had earned the right to discuss the resurrection of the dead. After Jesus rose, the angel at the tomb told the women, "Go, tell his disciples and Peter, 'He is going ahead of you into Galilee. There you will see him, just as he told you'" (Mark 16:7). Peter is specifically mentioned because Jesus knew Peter was filled with guilt and regret. That is why Peter had returned to his old profession—fishing in the Sea of Galilee. It was there, the place of his original calling, that Jesus met him again with the smell of a charcoal fire.

3. Willimon, *On a Dark and Windy Mountain*, 90.

Guest

Have you ever had a smell trigger some distinct memory in your life? Science tells us that our sense of smell (our olfactory sense) is closely linked to memory and can trigger both memories and feelings. A certain smell has the power to take you back to a specific time and place and resuscitate memories or feelings, for better or worse.

As Simon Peter wades to the shore, the smell of the charcoal fire transports him back to the night Jesus was arrested. The text is quite specific. John, the writer of the gospel, uses a word that is found only twice in the New Testament—*anthrakia*, a charcoal fire. The first use of anthrakia is in John 18:18 where Peter stood and warmed himself while denying that he ever knew Jesus:

> It was cold, and the servants and officials stood around a fire they had made to keep warm. Peter was there also standing with them, warming himself (John 18:18).

Dripping wet and empty-handed, Peter's nose carried him back to the events of that awful night. He had his shot at being a disciple and had failed miserably. It was impossible to believe that Jesus was still loving, calling, inviting, and forgiving him.

John 21 is best remembered for Jesus's threefold question: "Peter, do you love me?"

Peter affirms three times that indeed he does love Jesus and is told three times to go back to work feeding and tending the sheep—a threefold grace for a threefold denial. That grace is so baffling, so mystifying, and so limitless that any of us, regardless of our past or present, can find the strength to get up and try again. If Peter did, so can we.

Shortly before he died, John Lennon wrote a song for his young son, Sean. *Beautiful Boy* is a song about a father giving encouragement to his young son and includes this memorable line: "Life is what happens to you while you're busy making other plans." It is not just a great line; it is very true. Peter, because of his failure, was "busy making other plans" when Jesus came to invite him to be his guest for breakfast. Jesus is like Cracker Barrel. Breakfast is offered anytime of the day—anytime you need reminding that you will never out-sin the love of God.

4

Surrender

A certain ruler asked him, "Good teacher, what must I do to inherit eternal life?" "Why do you call me good?" Jesus answered. "No one is good—except God alone. You know the commandments: 'You shall not commit adultery, you shall not murder, you shall not steal, you shall not give false testimony, honor your father and mother.'" "All these I have kept since I was a boy," he said. When Jesus heard this, he said to him, "You still lack one thing. Sell everything you have and give to the poor, and you will have treasure in heaven. Then come, follow me." When he heard this, he became very sad, because he was very wealthy. Jesus looked at him and said, "How hard it is for the rich to enter the kingdom of God! Indeed, it is easier for a camel to go through the eye of a needle than for the rich to enter the kingdom of God." Those who heard this asked, "Who then can be saved?" Jesus replied, "What is impossible with human beings is possible with God." Peter said to him, "We have left all we had to follow you!" "Truly I tell you," Jesus said to them, "no one who has left home or wife or brothers or sisters or parents or children for the sake of the kingdom of God will fail to receive many times as much in this age, and in the age to come eternal life."

—LUKE 18:18–30

Faith is the heroic effort of your life. You fling yourself into reckless confidence on God. God has ventured all in Jesus to save us. Now he wants us to venture our all in a life that can face anything it has to face without wavering. Again, and again, you will get up to what Jesus wants, and every time you turn back when it comes to that point until you abandon resolutely. Jesus Christ demands that you risk everything that you hold by common sense—and leap into what he says. Christ demands of the man who trusts him the same reckless spirit that is daring enough to step out of the crowd and bank his faith on the character of God.

—OSWALD CHAMBERS

A DAIRY FARMER WENT to buy a new pickup truck. He had seen an advertisement in the paper offering tremendous discounts and factory rebates. He chose the new model he wanted and was ready to write the check.

The salesman said, "I'm sorry, sir, but I haven't calculated the price yet."

The farmer said, "What do you mean? Isn't the price what you advertised in the paper?"

The salesman said, "No, sir. That's the price for the basic model. All the options you chose on the truck cost extra."

The farmer was not happy but drove off in his new vehicle.

Months later, the car salesman volunteered to buy a cow for his son's 4-H project at school and remembered he had sold a truck to a dairy farmer some time back. He looked through his records, found the farmer's phone number, and gave him a call. The farmer said he would be glad to help him and would sell a good cow for five hundred dollars.

Later that week, the car salesman drove out to the farmer's place to pay for the cow.

After the farmer showed him the cow, the salesman handed him a check for five hundred dollars.

The farmer said, "I'm sorry, but I haven't given you the final cost yet. He then handed the salesman the following bill:

- Basic cow: $500
- Two-tone exterior: $45
- Extra stomach: $75
- Dual horns: $45
- Four handy spigots: $35
- Rear flyswatter: $100
- Natural fertilizer attachment: $200
- Grand total: $1,000

Whether we are buying cars or cows, it is always important to get to the bottom line.

What would you say the bottom line is when it comes to inheriting the kingdom of God? That is what the rich young ruler wanted to know when he posed his question to Jesus. He, like so many others, had come to believe that salvation is the product of one's behavior and beliefs. It is something we can somehow manipulate and control. We don't need God, except as the dispenser of the salvation we have earned ourselves. The question implies that we humans hold the initiative, as if God only acts at our behest when, in fact, a good God is always the initiator of unconditional love. Humans are merely the thankful recipients.

The rich young ruler prefaced his question by addressing Jesus as *good* teacher, but Jesus redirected his question to the goodness of God. Jesus was not refusing the title *good* teacher. He did not say,

Surrender

"Hey, I'm not good." In effect, he was saying, "My friend, the only one who you should be calling good is God himself, God alone."

Jesus pointed the young man to the Ten Commandments, which set the standard God requires:

> "You know the commandments: 'You shall not commit adultery, you shall not murder, you shall not steal, you shall not give false testimony, honor your father and mother'" (Luke 18:20).

Notice that Jesus quotes only five of the Ten Commandments. Why did Jesus choose just these five? To refresh our memory, here are the Ten Commandments (Exodus 20:3–17):

1. You shall have no other gods before me.
2. You shall not make yourself an idol.
3. You shall not take the Lord's name in vain.
4. Remember the Sabbath and keep it holy.
5. Honor your father and mother.
6. You shall not murder.
7. You shall not commit adultery.
8. You shall not steal.
9. You shall not bear false witness.
10. You shall not covet.

The first four commandments address our relationship with God. The remaining six address our relationship with family and others. Jesus, responding to this young man's question, skipped over the first four commandments and mentioned commandments five through nine—but not in the exact order.

I find that very interesting. If I were Jesus, and somebody asked me how to inherit eternal life, I would start with the first four commandments: "No other gods," "No idols," "No taking God's name in vain," and "Keep God's day holy." That is what I would do, but Jesus did not. Instead, he drew the young man's

Surrender

attention to the five commandments that deal with how one relates to other people.

The rich young ruler, thinking to himself, says, "I have done all of that since I was a kid." He had honored his mom and dad, he had not killed anyone, he had not committed adultery, and he had not stolen anything or lied in court.

Jesus was up to something. He was baiting the young man. "You still lack one thing . . . you're missing one thing." You can be sure Jesus had the attention of everyone around him.

I suppose the expression on the rich young man's face was a mixture of relief and expectancy. He probably thought, *Ok, only one thing, that's good. Just one more thing, and I'm heaven bound.*

That was when Jesus dropped the bomb: "Sell everything you have and give to the poor, and you will have treasure in heaven. Then come follow me" (Luke 18:22).

Silence. Dead silence. Nobody could believe what they had just heard. "When he heard this, he became very sad because he was very wealthy" (Luke 18:23). He turned his back on Jesus and walked away. End of story? Not quite.

Jesus's disciples were stunned. They thought, *If this guy cannot make it, who can? Here is a righteous man who took the law seriously and kept it and was rich!*

In that day, if you were rich, it was assumed that you had God's favor. It was sort of like the prosperity gospel that is so popular today. Obey the law, check the right boxes, put in your coin of faith, and out pops your health, wealth, and happiness from God's divine vending machine.

Jesus's encounter with this rich young ruler teaches something altogether different. God's favor is not attained by anything we do, but it is given to us freely as an act of grace. We need God to enable us to do what is impossible for us to do for ourselves: enter God's kingdom and inherit eternal life. Far too many of us are trying to earn God's approval, performing as well as we can and thinking if we can ever get our acts together, hopefully God will love and accept us. And all the while, we are not realizing perfect

Surrender

love meets us where we are and opens our hearts to receive the love for which we long.

We, like the rich young ruler, confuse surrender with obedience. As David G. Benner writes,

> The surrender Jesus invites from us—choosing his will and his life over our own—can never be motivated by anything but love. But we can and frequently do offer a substitute for surrender—something that looks superficially enough like it that we easily confuse it with surrender. We can offer obedience. For many Christians obedience is more familiar than surrender. The Bible never uses the term surrender apart from a military context, while it repeatedly encourages obedience. Not surprisingly, therefore, sermons and popular Christian writing typically also focus on obedience. By contrasting obedience and surrender I do not want to put too much distance between them. Those who surrender obey. But not all who obey surrender. It is quite easy to obey God for the wrong reasons. What God desires is submission of our heart and will, not simply compliance in our behavior.[1]

Inheriting eternal life involves saying yes to Jesus *and* saying no to self. Surrendering one's life to Jesus is a life of death to the kingdom of self. Self-interest suffocates life, but the love of God connects us to life, a life we no longer control.

> No longer can I choose whom I will love and whom I will ignore. No longer can I close my eyes to the things that hold others in bondage. For if God's heart has truly become mine, their bondage is mine. If one person suffers, all suffer (1 Corinthians 12:26). I may not always consciously experience the suffering of others. I may be reasonably successful in living the lie of autonomous existence. But my identity is based on an illusion unless it is grounded in human solidarity and community.[2]

---

1. Benner, *Surrender to Love*, 55.
2. Benner, *Surrender to Love*, 94.

Surrender

Accepting Jesus's invitation to "take up [our] cross and follow [him]" (Matthew 16:24) is not only about trying to be a better person. Being a follower of Christ is about more than being a better humanitarian. In following Christ, we soon realize Jesus's invitation does not come with a promise of protection from life's trials. Facing life's trials will eventually shake our world, leading to a genuine faith that inspires and empowers us to go all the way. We trade our agendas and expectations for God's agenda and mystery. It is mystery that frightens us most.

William Borden was an heir to the Borden estate when he graduated from high school in 1904. For his graduation present, his parents gave him a trip around the world. On his trip, he felt a growing burden for the world's suffering people. He later wrote home and said, "I plan on surrendering my life to the cause of world missions." At the same time, he wrote two words in the back of his Bible: "No reserves."

Holding nothing back, he became a pillar in Yale University's Christian student organization. One entry in his journal demonstrated the source of his spiritual strength: "Say no to self and yes to Jesus every time."

While at Yale, William Borden started a small prayer group that would transform campus life. By the end of his freshman year, 150 students were meeting for weekly Bible study and prayer. By the end of his senior year, one thousand of Yale's 1,300 students were meeting in such groups. Borden's real passion was missions, and he narrowed his missionary call to the Kansu people in China.[3]

Upon graduation, Borden wrote two more words in the back of his Bible: "No retreats." Because of his call and commitment, Borden refused positions in his family's business as well as several other high-paying job offers, enrolling in seminary instead. Upon graduating from seminary, he immediately went to Egypt to learn Arabic to work with Muslims in China. While in Egypt, he contracted spinal meningitis. In less than a month, the twenty-five-year-old William Borden was dead. When his family opened his Bible, they discovered he had written two more words.

---

3. Taylor, *Borden of Yale '09*, 150.

Surrender

Underneath the words "No reserves" and "No retreats," he had written "No regrets."[4]

We may not understand God's ways, but we know his heart because he revealed it perfectly in Jesus Christ. Because of Jesus Christ, we know God is for us, we know God can be trusted, and we know God's way is always best whether we understand it or not. Our security is not in what God is doing but in who God is. It sometimes strains our faith to affirm that, but it is nonetheless true.

We are sometimes like the farmer who had a fine ewe that gave birth to two lambs. When one lamb died, the farmer remarked, "Well, I'd rather have one fat lamb than two skinny ones." Then the other lamb died, and the farmer said, "Well, it is all for the best, I guess. Now the mother won't be bothered by two little ones and can look after herself." A week later, the mother died. The farmer, trying to remain positive, shook his head and said, "Well, I'm sure that it's all for the best, but for the life of me, I can't figure it out."

I can appreciate how this farmer felt. Why God allows certain things to happen when we are in the center of his will is beyond me. But this I do know: he is a good God, telling a good story that will have a good ending. I can trust surrendering to his plan and the love he has for me. Because all power in heaven and earth has been given to Jesus (Matthew 28:18), ultimately, all will turn out well, every problem will be solved, every blighting effect of evil will be erased, and all wrongs will be righted.

Peter, unlike the rich young ruler, turned his back on everything to follow Christ. Surrendering to love, he was assured by love incarnate that he would not regret his leap of faith:

> Peter said to him, "We have left all we had to follow you!"
> "Truly I tell you," Jesus said to them, "No one who has left home or wife or brothers or sisters or parents or children for the sake of the kingdom of God will fail to receive many times as much in this age, and in the age to come eternal life" (Luke 18:28–30).

---

4. Taylor, *Borden of Yale '09*, 150.

Surrender

Peter, who began life in the fishing village of Capernaum, ended up taking the gospel across Asia and Europe before being martyred in Rome. That is what it meant for Peter to follow Jesus. It cost him a lot to surrender to love, and it will cost us a lot as well. According to Jesus, it will cost us everything:

> Suppose one of you wants to build a tower. Won't you first sit down and estimate the cost to see if you have enough money to complete it? For if you lay the foundation and are not able to finish it, everyone who sees it will ridicule you, saying, "This person began to build and wasn't able to finish." Or suppose a king is about to go to war against another king. Won't he first sit down and consider whether he is able with ten thousand men to oppose the one coming against him with twenty thousand? If he is not able, he will send a delegation while the other is still a long way off and will ask for terms of peace. In the same way, those of you who do not give up everything you have cannot be my disciples (Luke 14:28–33).

Like committed soldiers fighting to the finish, followers of Christ must be willing to give it their all, trusting thoroughly the one to whom they have committed themselves. Be warned though: when you side with Jesus, expect the unexpected!

5

Children

People were also bringing babies to Jesus for him to place his hands on them. When the disciples saw this, they rebuked them. But Jesus called the children to him and said, "Let the little children come to me, and do not hinder them, for the kingdom of God belongs to such as these. Truly I tell you, anyone who will not receive the kingdom of God like a little child will never enter it."

—Luke 18:15–17

Our religion is one which challenges the ordinary human standards by holding that the ideal of life is the spirit of a little child. We tend to glorify adulthood and wisdom and worldly prudence, but the gospel reverses all this. The gospel says that the inescapable condition of entrance into the divine fellowship is that we turn and become as a little child. As against our natural judgment we must become tender and full of wonder and unspoiled by the hard skepticism on which we so often pride ourselves. But when we really look

Children

into the heart of a child, willful as they may be, we are often ashamed. God has sent children into the world, not only to replenish it, but to serve as sacred reminders of something ineffably precious which we are always in danger of losing. The sacrament of childhood is thus a continuing revelation.

—Elton Trueblood

WILLIAM WILLIMON, A BISHOP in the United Methodist Church and former dean of Duke Chapel in North Carolina, told the story about rushing his family into the car on a cold Christmas Eve. They were running late for the Christmas Eve Communion service, and on their way to church, hindered by heavy traffic, their five-year-old daughter got sick and threw up all over the car.

Great, William Willimon thought, *if people only knew what preachers go through on their way to church.* He wheeled into the church parking lot, jumped out of the car, and left his wife, Patsy, to clean up the mess and get the kids into church.

Patsy, leading a still unsteady and pale Harriet into the church, sought the back pew in the darkness, just in case Harriet got sick again. The Willimons' son, William Jr., age seven, ran down to the front of the church to sit with his grandparents.

Will Willimon threw on his robe, took a deep breath, and joined the choir for the processional. He made it through the first part of the service and the sermon. Then came Communion. Patsy came down to the altar to receive the bread and cup, having left sick little Harriet on the back pew.

Then something beautiful happened. Seven-year-old William Jr. got up and came back to the communion table. *What on earth is he doing?* wondered the parents and grandparents. *He has already received Communion once. What is he doing?*

Young William walked discreetly to the back of the church and scooted down the pew toward his sick little sister. He opened his hand, revealing a small piece of juice-stained bread, and said, "Harriet, the body and blood of Christ given for you."

Children

Without hesitation, little Harriet picked the bread out of her brother's hand, popped it into her mouth, and whispered, "Amen." And in that moment, Communion had never been more holy.[1]

Jesus, recognizing all that children teach us, reprimanded his disciples for chasing away their professors:

> Let the little children come to me, and do not hinder them, for the kingdom of God belongs to such as these (Luke 18:16).

Why did the disciples do this? Perhaps they were trying to protect Jesus's time and space. Perhaps they resented the noise or chaos in having so many children around. Whatever their motivation, they learned that day that childlikeness and authentic faith go hand in hand.

With that in mind, let us consider three great lessons our children teach us: First, our children teach us that we do not need to be religiously domesticated. Do you remember the excitement you felt when you began your journey with Jesus? You did not know all the rules, but that was OK because you knew the Lord of all rules.

Every time the disciples started throwing around rules—No children near Jesus!—No talking to wayward women in public!—Quit wasting expensive perfume!—Jesus told them to knock it off.

How many spend their lives concerned with learning what they cannot do instead of celebrating all they can do in the freedom we have in Christ? It was Jesus who touched lepers, which was against the rules. It was Jesus who did what he pleased on the Sabbath, which was against the rules. It was Jesus who forgave and loved people instead of stoning them, which was against the rules. Rules were given for one purpose and one purpose only: to lead us to grace.

Although scripture began with a mountain of "shall nots," it always moved toward grace—always! A recent meme on Facebook has gone viral and for good reason since it celebrates the marvelous march of grace:

---

1. Willimon, *Stories by Willimon*, 68–69.

Children

> The Bible is clear: Moabites are bad. They were not allowed to dwell among God's people (Deuteronomy 23). But then comes the story of Ruth the Moabite, which challenges the prejudice against Moabites. (Ruth is an ancestress of Jesus)
>
> The Bible is clear: People from Uz are evil (Jeremiah 25). But then comes the story of Job, a man from Uz, who was the most blameless man on earth.
>
> The Bible is clear: No foreigners or Eunuchs allowed (Deuteronomy 23). But then comes the story of an African eunuch welcomed into the church (Acts 8).
>
> The Bible is clear: God's people hated Samaritans. But then Jesus tells the story of a Good Samaritan (Luke 10).
>
> The Bible may begin with prejudice, discrimination, and animosity, but the spirit moves God's people toward openness, welcome, inclusion, acceptance, and affirmation.[2]

Childlike faith is diving headlong into the liberating grace of Jesus Christ. It is a synergy of childlike trust and hope and unpretentiousness that knows our Good Shepherd will lead us into paths of righteousness for his name's sake. Which is better: a map or a human guide?

Childlike trust is carefree, spontaneous, imaginative, joyful, and playful. According to Jesus, this is the only way to enter and experience the kingdom of God. Jesus is not the rule-maker; he is the rule-overcomer. He is the one and only ruler.

A second thing that children teach us is that we must love passionately with all our hearts, souls, and minds. Children love their fathers and mothers passionately, and Jesus is saying we should love our heavenly parent with that same kind of passion. God wants your love more than anything else. Never forget that.

Mike Yaconelli tells the story of a young father, a typical type A personality, who followed the same routine every workday. He would arrive home around five thirty, park the car in the garage, enter the house, place his briefcase in the hallway, and go into the

---

2. Bixby Knolls Christian Church, Facebook Post.

Children

kitchen. Once in the kitchen, he would open a cabinet, take out a glass, and place it on the counter. He would then open the fridge, take out a carton of milk, and pour himself a full glass. Then he would grab a cookie from the cookie jar on the counter, walk down to the den, and sit down to watch the news.

One night, this young father came home from work and began his usual routine. As he stepped into the hallway, setting down his briefcase, he saw his little son standing down the hall with a smile on his face (obviously anticipating his father's return). Daddy knew something was up and he stopped and watched his son turn around and head for the kitchen.

Pleasantly surprised, Dad crept to the edge of the kitchen to see what his little fellow was up to. The little boy ran to the corner of the kitchen, pulled out the bottom drawer, which he was not supposed to do, stepped on the drawer, climbed up on the counter, which he was not supposed to do, and pulled out a glass, knocking the other glasses over. Thankfully, none of them broke.

With glass in hand, the little boy scooted back down onto the drawer, then to the floor, and then over to the cookie jar, knocking it over and spilling the cookies all over the floor. Oblivious to his father, he scooped up all the cookies and placed them on the counter, except for one.

Picking up the cookie, he ran over to the refrigerator, placed the cookie and empty glass on the floor, opened the refrigerator door, and reached inside, grabbing the half-gallon container of milk. Awfully heavy for a five-year-old, it promptly fell to the floor, which knocked off the top, spilling a little milk. He then picked up the container of milk, and wobbling terribly, he attempted to pour the milk into the glass, spilling milk all over the floor.

Any other evening, the father would have yelled at his son by this time, pointing out the terrible mess he was making. Instead, he sensed something much more important was happening here. He patiently waited as his little boy picked up the cookie and glass of milk and came running to him with the biggest smile on his

Children

face. The father threw his arms around his son and thanked him for such a wonderful surprise.[3]

The five-year-old had done what he did out of passion for his father, and fortunately, his father had recognized it. Normally by the time little boys are five, their spontaneity and passion have been squelched out of them, and by the time they are big boys, it is a forgotten luxury of childhood.

As you read this story, I am sure voices of neatness, order, tidiness, and responsibility were screaming, "Do not step on the drawer! Get off the counter! Look out, you are going to break all those glasses! Look at that mess you have made on the floor! You are spilling milk everywhere!" Had this father listened to those voices, who knows what damage would have been done to his son. But the passion of this little boy drew out the passion of his father, and his only response was gratitude.

There were times in my early faith journey when I pictured God standing at the door of the kitchen saying, "Richard, put the glass down! Stop doing that! Get off the counter! Look at the mess you have made!" I had no idea that as I stumbled up to God with my milk and cookie in hand, God was grateful, mess and all, opening his arms and saying, "Thank you, son. Your passion pleases me. Thank you for wanting to please me."

In those early years of my religious life, I was taught that God loves me, but it seemed that the good news was buffered by what felt like bad news. It was a concoction of grace and works. It took me far too long to accept the outrageous too-good-to-believe news that God's love is unearned, extravagant, undeserved, and irresistible. It took a while for me to accept the truth that the God of all creation loves me with no conditions and no fine print.

As much as I was passionate about God, it was hard to believe he was passionate about me. But now, years later, having walked with him, having experienced his love and faithfulness, I know that he is for me and not against me. I know he loves me beyond my understanding. Children teach us to love with abandon, with

---

3. Yaconelli, *Dangerous Wonder*, 113–14.

Children

unbridled passion, and if we do love this way, the messes will take care of themselves.

A final thing that children can teach us is that the nature of God is sometimes playful. When you were a kid, did you like to play hide-and-seek? Our Father God hides sometimes. Over the course of our lives, we will find him in places we never thought he would be. Sometimes he hides in difficulties, sometimes he hides in suffering, sometimes he hides in good times and bad, and sometimes he hides in the stories of our lives. Whatever our circumstances, whatever our status, God is present, hiding, waiting for us to discover him, and waiting for us to learn from him in the shadows as well as the light.

He also chooses to hide himself in those for whom there is no room. Thomas Merton reminds us:

> Into this world, this demented inn, in which there is absolutely no room for him at all, Christ has come uninvited. But because he cannot be at home in it, because he is out of place in it, and yet he must be in it, his place is with those others for whom there is no room. His place is with those who do not belong, who are rejected by power because they are regarded as weak, those who are discredited, who are denied the status of persons, tortured, exterminated. With those for whom there is no room, Christ is present in the world. He is mysteriously present in those for whom there seems to be nothing but the world at its worst. It is in these that he hides himself, for whom there is no room.[4]

God is love doing what love does. He loves losing himself in something or someone, inviting those of us who are willing to play, to join him in a game of hide-and-seek.

The late Catholic priest, Henri Nouwen, wrote a wonderful book for his nephew, Marc. *Letters to Marc About Jesus*, a small seven-chapter book, has one letter entitled "The Hidden God." In this particular letter, Nouwen says God rarely works where we think God works, namely in and through well-known

---

4. Merton, *Raids on the Unspeakable*, 72–73.

Children

public figures. Instead, he usually works in ways we often overlook, through the marginalized (like children) or those with little power or influence:

> God prefers to work in secret. You must have the nerve to let the mystery of God's secrecy, God's anonymity, sink deeply into your consciousness because otherwise, you're continually looking in the wrong direction . . . maybe while we focus our whole attention on the VIPs and their movements, on peace conferences and protest demonstrations, it is totally unknown people, praying and working in silence, who make God save us yet again from destruction . . . Perhaps the very greatest of saints remain anonymous (like the children to whom the kingdom is promised).[5]

No doubt, Jesus encountered many children throughout his life and ministry. He delighted in their simple faith and understood their needs, their fears, and the challenges of living in such an unpredictable and dangerous world. Scripture tells us that Jesus took little ones into his arms and even used a child's lunch to feed more than five thousand people. As the beloved hymn says, "Jesus loves the little children." He invites all to live in that knowledge, knowing we are—and forever will be children of God—secure in his love.

---

5. Nouwen, *Letters to Marc about Jesus*, 68.

6

Peacemaking

While he was still speaking a crowd came up, and the man who was called Judas, one of the Twelve, was leading them. He approached Jesus to kiss him, but Jesus asked him, "Judas are you betraying the Son of Man with a kiss?" When Jesus's followers saw what was going to happen, they said, "Lord, should we strike with our swords?" And one of them struck the servant of the high priest, cutting off his right ear. But Jesus answered, "No more of this!" And he touched the man's ear and healed him.

—Luke 22:47–51

Then Simon Peter, who had a sword, drew it and struck the high priest's servant, cutting off his right ear. (The servant's name was Malchus).

—John 18:10

> *Peacemaking*
>
> What Jesus did to embody the will of the Father on the cross was not just done on our behalf; it was also done as the way we are to follow. Jesus did not renounce the way of violence for the way of peace so that we could renounce the way of peace for the way of violence. The long dark night of mankind's addiction to violence has come to an end. The new day of Messiah's peace has dawned, and we are called to be children of the day. Do we dare?
>
> —Brian Zahnd

On the evening of June 17, 2015, a young man named Dylann Roof walked into a Bible study at Mother Emanuel AME Church in Charleston, South Carolina. This young white man received a warm welcome from the African American parishioners of this historic congregation. To them, he was a welcomed visitor.

However, after receiving a warm welcome, Dylann Roof took out an automatic weapon and opened fire on the church members, taking nine innocent lives. This mass murder shocked the nation, a horrifying story of a delusional young white supremacist who was welcomed into a Wednesday evening Bible study only to pull out a gun and murder nine of his gracious hosts.

The response of several of the victim's relatives at Dylann Roof's bail hearing two days later shocked the nation again: expressions of forgiveness from grieving family members. Nadine Collier, whose mother was murdered, had not planned on expressing forgiveness at the hearing because she didn't know she would even have a chance to speak. Addressing Dylann Roof directly, she said, "I forgive you. You took something very precious away from me. I will never get to talk to my mother again, but I forgive you and may God have mercy on your soul. You hurt me. You hurt a lot of people. If God forgives you then I forgive you."

Anthony Thompson lost his wife, Myra, that night, and he stood up in the courtroom and urged Dylann Roof to repent and turn to Jesus, adding, "So that no matter what happens to you, you'll be OK."[1]

People like Nadine Collier and Anthony Thompson leave most of us wondering how. How can they offer forgiveness for such a heinous crime? How can they stand in a courtroom two days later and offer God's grace? There can be only one answer. They offered grace because having received grace themselves, they were under a higher law, the law of love.

Don't we pray this every time we pray the prayer taught to us by Jesus?

And forgive us our debts, as we have also forgiven our debtors.

The grace we have received is the grace we are to give to others. This is our calling as kingdom people.

The very last miracle Jesus performed was a miracle of grace. It was on the night he was betrayed, and it seems small compared to his other miracles like walking on water or raising the dead. But was it? This is the only account we have in scripture of a healing miracle following an act of violence. Perhaps the real miracle was not that Jesus healed the man but that he wanted to under such circumstances:

> And one of them struck the servant of the high priest, cutting off his right ear. But Jesus answered, "No more of this!" And he touched the man's ear and healed him (Luke 22:50–51).

When it comes to peacemaking and extending the grace we have received, there are at least three lessons we learn from Jesus's last miracle. First, Jesus's last miracle shows us how to respond to our enemies. Jesus taught us much about loving those who do not love us. We should love them, feed them, forgive them, refuse to retaliate, turn the other cheek, and pray for them:

"Whoever claims to live in him must live as Jesus did" (1 John 2:6).

---

1. Von Drehle et al., "Murder, Race and Mercy," 43–68.

Peacemaking

If we are to walk like Jesus walked, we must demonstrate a new paradigm, one that loves the enemy mainly because God also loves them.

In Paul's letter to the Ephesians, we see that God is the ultimate peacemaker:

> For he himself is our peace, who has made the two one and who has destroyed the barrier, the dividing wall of hostility, by setting aside in his flesh the law with its commands and regulations. His purpose was to create in himself one new humanity out of the two, thus making peace, and in one body to reconcile both of them to God through the cross, by which he put to death their hostility. He came and preached peace to you who were far away and peace to those who were near (Ephesians 2:14–17).

On the night of Jesus's last miracle, the only one who remembered how God expects us to act was Jesus. The Jewish leaders were blind to God, Judas had turned his back on God, and his disciples seemed to have forgotten God. But Jesus remembered.

If we are honest, there is a part of us that admires what Peter did that night. There is something within us that likes the notion of repaying evil with evil. Something stimulating, invigorating, instinctive. It is something very human.

Thinking violence will rid the world of violence is a very human thing, not a divine thing. In *A Farewell to Mars*, Brian Zahnd agrees:

> Jesus did not tell his oppressed hearers not to resist evil. That would be absurd . . . A proper translation of Jesus's teaching would then be, "Don't strike back at evil (or, one who has done you evil) in kind. Do not retaliate against violence with violence." The scholar's version is brilliant: "Don't react violently against the one who is evil." Jesus was no less committed to opposing evil than the anti-Roman resistance fighters. The only difference was over the means to be used: how one should fight evil. There are three general responses to evil: (1) passivity (2) violent

opposition, and (3) the third way of militant nonviolence articulated by Jesus.[2]

Being a peacemaker will never be easy. It will come at a cost and is never passive. Think of Jesus and the woman caught in the act of adultery. He stepped between the woman and the Pharisees and bore the heat of their aggression on her behalf. Defending the terrified woman at his feet, he met the murderous mob with an alternate form of power, suffering love on behalf of the oppressed. There was no violence in Jesus, only unfathomable love undercutting the age-old human tendency to label those outside a privileged circle as enemies, adversaries, or transgressors:

> A South African woman stood in an emotionally charged courtroom listening to white police officers acknowledge the atrocities they had perpetrated in the name of apartheid. The Officer Van de Broek confessed to the death of her son. Along with others he had shot the eighteen-year-old at point-blank range and burned his body, turning it over and over until it was reduced to ashes.
>
> Eight years later, Van de Broek also seized this same woman's husband and bound him. She was forced to watch as they poured gasoline over his body and set him on fire. The last words she heard her husband say were, "Forgive them."
>
> Now Van de Broek stood before this woman awaiting judgment and sentencing. The court of the Reconciliation Commission asked her what she wanted his punishment to be. Here is what she said:
>
> I want three things. I want Mr. Van de Broek to take me to the place where they buried my husband's body. I would like to gather up the dust and give him a decent burial.
>
> Second: Mr. Van de Broek took all my family away from me, and I still have a lot to give. Twice a month I would like him to come to the ghetto and spend a day with me so I can be a mother to him.
>
> Third: I would like Mr. Van de Broek to know that God will forgive him as I have. I would like someone to

---

2. Zahnd, *A Farewell to Mars*, 10–11.

> help me over to where he is seated so that I can embrace him, and he will know my forgiveness is real.
>
> As the elderly woman was led across the courtroom Van de Broek fainted. Someone started singing Amazing Grace and gradually everyone joined in.[3]

A second thing Jesus's last miracle teaches us is that love cares for even the smallest things. Sherlock Holmes said, "To a great mind, nothing is small." Imagine how many things Jesus must have had on his mind there in Gethsemane. He had been betrayed by one of his own, and he would soon endure a mock trial that would lead to a death none of us can imagine. Yet Jesus takes the time to meet the need of the one who has come to arrest him:

> To a great mind nothing is small. The number of hairs on your head, a little sparrow falling to the ground, little children and what they teach us. The same is true when it comes to peacemaking. Even the smallest act can grow into something very significant. Take Brennan Manning for example. In the Atlanta airport, he was having his shoes shined by an elderly black man when the Spirit of God spoke to his heart. As soon as the elderly black man had finished, Brennan Manning paid him and gave him a very generous tip, but he did not stop there. Looking at the elderly man who had just shined his shoes, he said, "Now sir, you sit down in the chair because I want to shine your shoes." "You're going to do what?" the elderly man said. "I want to shine your shoes," Manning said. "Come on now, sit on down and teach me how to do it well." As Brennan Manning began to shine the old man's shoes, the old man began to weep and said, "No white man has ever treated me this way." They parted with a strong hug.[4]

Small things done in love can accomplish great things. Several years ago, I read about pastors, black and white, who met weekly in Birmingham, Alabama, to pray for their city. *What a great idea*, I thought—and then I remembered I did not even know the black

---

3. Green, "Canadian Mennonite," In *1001 Illustrations That Connect*, 85.
4. Buhler, "The Ultimate Community," Tape No. 146.

pastor whose church was less than two football fields from my own. I felt convicted for never having reached out to him and decided to invite him to lunch.

When we met, waiting for our food, I said, "Calvin, I want to ask your forgiveness. I have been here three years and have never reached out to you, my brother pastor."

Calvin looked at me intently and said, "No, my brother, I was already here when you arrived. I should have welcomed you first, so please forgive me." From that day, we have been close friends. Our congregations worship together on special occasions like Dr. King's birthday in January, and we also jointly participate in ministry to our city. For fifteen years, we have shared ministry together, and it all began with one little phone call.

A final thing that Jesus's last miracle teaches is that love will have the final move. I have always been moved by the lyrics of George Matheson's beautiful hymn *O Love that Wilt Not Let Me Go*.

> Oh love that wilt not let me go
> I rest my weary soul in Thee
> I give Thee back the life I owe,
> That in Thine ocean depths its flow
> May richer, fuller be.

Norman Vincent Peale certainly believed that love has the final move. *The Power of Positive Thinking* is one of the best-selling books of the twentieth century. When his book was published, Peale was attacked from all sides. Liberals did not like him because he was too conservative, emphasizing prayer, Bible study, and salvation in Christ alone. Conservatives did not like him because they did not think he talked enough about sin, hell, and God's wrath.

But over the years, in all his writings and public speaking, he never countered the attacks. He never felt it necessary to defend himself. When Peale was in his nineties, someone made the comment that he had outlived his enemies. A friend of his who knew him well said, "No, Norman didn't outlive his enemies, he out-loved them."[5]

---

5. Peale, *The True Joy of Positive Living*, 154.

Peacemaking

The great Chicago preacher, D. L. Moody, sums things up well:

> I can imagine Jesus saying one day, "Go find the man who put the crown of thorns on my brow; tell him I have a crown for him in my kingdom. Find the man who smote my head with a reed, driving thorns deeper into my brow; tell him I want to give him a scepter (an emblem of royal authority). Go seek that poor soldier who drove the spear into my side; tell him there is a nearer way to my heart."[6]

Because God is love, love will always have the final move.

---

6. Moody Fitt, *Day by Day with D. L. Moody*, "Devotional for April 19."

7

Doubt

On the evening of that first day of the week, when the disciples were together, with the doors locked for fear of the Jewish leaders, Jesus came and stood among them and said, "Peace be with you!" After he said this, he showed them his hands and side. The disciples were overjoyed when they saw the Lord. Again, Jesus said, "Peace be with you! As the Father has sent me, I am sending you." And with that he breathed on them and said, "Receive the Holy Spirit. If you forgive anyone's sins, their sins are forgiven; if you do not forgive them, they are not forgiven." Now Thomas (also known as Didymus), one of the Twelve, was not with the disciples when Jesus came. So, the other disciples told him, "We have seen the Lord!" But he said to them, "Unless I see the nail marks in his hands and put my finger where the nails were, and put my hand into his side, I will not believe." A week later his disciples were in the house again, and Thomas was with them. Though the doors were locked, Jesus came and stood among them and said, "Peace be with you!" Then he said to Thomas, "Put your finger here; see my hands. Reach out your hand and put it into my side. Stop doubting and believe."

Doubt

> Thomas said to him, "My Lord and my God!" Then Jesus told him, "Because you have seen me, you have believed; blessed are those who have not seen and yet have believed."
>
> —John 20:19–29

> The minute we begin to think we know all the answers, we forget the questions, and we become smug like the Pharisee who listed all his considerable virtues, and thanked God that he was not like other men ... Those who believe in God, but without passion of the heart, without anguish of mind, without uncertainty, without doubt, and even at times without despair, believe only in the idea of God, and not in God himself.
>
> —Madeleine L'Engle

After retiring from a long and fruitful ministry, famed pastor William Sloane Coffin penned his final book, a wonderful little book entitled *Letters to a Young Doubter*. He imagined a young college student struggling with doubts and confusion about his faith as well as difficulties in his personal life. With college professors challenging this young man's most cherished beliefs, Coffin wrote these words of encouragement:

> That's what professors do, some with a little too much relish. But don't be anxious about your newfound doubts. Doubts move you forward not backward, just as long as you doubt out of love of the truth, not out of pathological need to doubt. In searching for new truths, don't insist on absolute intellectual certainty.[1]

I needed a letter like this when I began my journey with Jesus all those years ago, and I am guessing you did too.

---

1. Coffin, *Letters to a Young Doubter*, 2.

Doubt

We people of faith can get stuck obsessing on facts and certainty—ten proofs for this or five reasons to never doubt that—instead of easing into the reality of never being able to know some things. Perhaps, like me, you have trouble reconciling all the suffering in the world with a loving God, an eternal hell where souls are tortured forever, or seeing people you love experience life in such a way that it kicks the legs of belief right out from under you.

When we struggle with doubt, what exactly we are doubting? Is it God or our ideas about God? In a growing faith, doubts are inevitable because we can never trap God into words, concepts, creeds, or doctrines. He will always be beyond, and we must never confuse our theological constructs with God because theological constructs only take us so far if it is truly God that we are seeking.

Doubt can be healthy if it is done in a certain way, out of love for truth. That is why I am thankful for people in the Bible like Thomas who would not believe Jesus rose from the dead until he saw for himself. Instead of pretending doubt was not present, he brought it out into the light to be examined. If hidden and suppressed, doubt can fester in the heart and poison the soul.

Catholic theologian Richard Rohr argues that we should even welcome doubt and mystery:

> If you think you have a right to certitude, then show me where the Gospel ever promised or offered you that. If God wanted us to have evidence, rational proof, and perfect clarity, the incarnation of Jesus would have been delayed until the invention of audio recorders and video cameras.
>
> Rational certitude is exactly what the scriptures do not offer us. They offer us something much better and an entirely different way of knowing: an intimate relationship, a dark journey, a path where we must discover for ourselves that grace, love, mercy, and forgiveness are absolutely necessary for survival in an uncertain world. You only need enough clarity and ground to know how to live without certitude! Yes, we really are saved by faith. People who live in this way never stop growing, are not easily defeated, and frankly, are fun to live with.

Doubt

> You can tell mature and authentic faith by people's ability to deal with darkness, failure, and non-validation of the ego—and by their quiet but confident joy! Infantile religion insists on certainty every step of the way and thus is not very happy.[2]

There will come a time in each of our lives when desire for clarity will collide with unfulfilled expectations. Mike Tyson once said, "Everybody has a plan until they get punched in the mouth." This is what happened to John the Baptist. Languishing in prison, he had been punched in the mouth, figuratively speaking, for preaching uncomfortable truths about King Herod Antipas's adulterous relationship with his half-brother Phillip's wife (Matthew 14).

From prison, under such conditions, John sent his disciples to Jesus asking, "Are you the one who is to come, or shall I look for another?" In other words, "Are you really the Messiah? If you are the Messiah, and all I have said about you is true, then why do the Herods of the world seem to have the upper hand? Why is this happening to me? Could I have been wrong about you?" If the greatest man born of woman (Luke 7:28) struggled with doubt when Jesus did not meet his expectations, you can be sure we will as well.

John's questions are not indicative of his having lost faith; instead, he is seeking something in which to place his trust and his hope. When we don't understand the events that take place in our lives, or twists and turns in our faith journey, we can still be at peace, trusting radically that God's story is still unfolding and will take us where we need to go. Our call allows us to express not only our hopes and dreams but also our fears and doubts. We can rest in knowing that in every circumstance, God's faithfulness will always be stronger than our uncertainty and doubt.

One of my favorite stories about being too sure of ourselves and rigid in our convictions is the true story Bishop Fulton Sheen once told about himself. Bishop Sheen was one of the first TV preachers back in the 1950s. One day, he was riding on a subway in New York. At one stop, a disreputable-looking gentleman, reeking

---

2. Rohr and Morrell, *The Divine Dance*, 100–101.

of booze and body odor, boarded the subway and plopped down in the seat next to Bishop Sheen.

Turning to Bishop Sheen, he asked, "How does a man get diabetes?"

Figuring this was his chance to rebuke this man, Bishop Sheen responded sarcastically, "A man gets diabetes from drinking too much and neglecting his responsibilities." As soon as the words were out of his mouth, the good bishop experienced remorse. *I should not have put this man down like that*, he thought. To restart the conversation, Bishop Sheen turned to the man and asked, "Tell me, why did you ask me that question?"

The man, looking up with bloodshot eyes, replied, "I just heard that the pope has diabetes."[3]

Being too rigid in our convictions is spiritually unhealthy. What we think we know keeps us from knowing what there is to know. It is wholesome to rethink our thoughts, reform our ideas, and revise our beliefs because if anything is true about God, it is that God will not always be who we say God is. Theologically, we need to be light on our feet and loose in our saddles:

> "For my thoughts are not your thoughts, neither are your ways, my ways," declares the Lord. "As the heavens are higher than the earth, so are my ways higher than your ways and my thoughts than your thoughts" (Isaiah 55:8–9).

In *Wrestling with God: Stories of Doubt and Faith*, longtime reporter Barbara Newhall learned that the gap between life experience and faith is necessary for spiritual growth. Pregnant with her daughter, she realized one day she could not feel the baby moving inside. On her way to have an ultrasound, she refused to beg God because she wanted nothing to do with any God cruel enough to take away babies and spare them on a whim.

When Newhall's healthy baby kicked in irritation to the ultrasound tech's movements, she couldn't bring herself to "thank God for my daughter's life any more than I had been able to ask for it

---

3. Sheen, *Treasure the Clay*, 324.

earlier. How could I thank God for something God had so nearly taken from me, and so gratuitously? God—and the universe I was born into—was not to be trusted."[4]

But despite her doubts, Newhall continued attending church because she felt something missing from her life, something big. She went there "hoping that God, too, would show up in some tangible, concrete way, bringing reassurance that yes, a loving intentional force was at work in the universe, and that yes, I mattered."[5]

Barbara Newhall would eventually conclude that even though uncertainty and doubt are frustrating, the gap between experience and faith is fertile territory where important things are birthed and grow into even more important things. Certainty very often leaves little room for spiritual growth and little room for the spiritual struggle that formed the faith of so many of our spiritual ancestors.

Perhaps we have put too much emphasis on faith as a noun, something we possess or do not possess. Faith can also be a verb—keeping at it, sticking with it, wrestling with the hard questions, and waiting. That is what pastor and author Barbara Brown Taylor found herself having to do:

> By the time I had resigned as pastor from Grace Calvary Church, I had arrived at an understanding of faith that had far more to do with trust than with certainty. I trusted God to be God even if I could not say who God was for sure. I trusted God to sustain the world although I could not say for sure how it happened. I trusted God to hold me and those I loved, in life and in death, without giving me one shred of conclusive evidence that it was so . . . This understanding had the welcome effect of changing faith from a noun to a verb for me.[6]

It seems the best thing to do with doubt is to welcome it, embrace it, and ask it what it can teach us.

There is a difference between doubt and unbelief. Doubt is "I *cannot* believe." Unbelief is "I *will not* believe." Doubt is honesty;

4. Newhall, *Wrestling with God*, 75–76.
5. Newhall, *Wrestling with God*, 76.
6. Brown Taylor, *Leaving Church*, 170.

unbelief is obstinacy. Doubt is looking for light; unbelief is being content with darkness. Our Lord understood that once Thomas worked through his doubts, he would be one of the surest men in the early church. Maybe it was the Lord who inspired Alfred Lord Tennyson to write, "There lives more faith in honest doubt than in half the creeds."

The disciple Thomas's bout with doubt was certainly not the end of his story. Remember the parable of the shepherd who left ninety-nine to go out and search for the one lost sheep? That is exactly the Jesus we see in John 20. Lovingly and patiently, the risen Shepherd seeks out his lost sheep and transforms the misery of his descending doubts to the blessedness of a living faith:

> Put your finger here; see my hands. Reach out your hand and put it into my side. Stop doubting and believe (John 20:27).

Tradition has it that after Christ's ascension, Thomas became a missionary to India. Being a faithful follower of Jesus Christ, he was later martyred there. A man paralyzed by doubt would never have come to such an ending. Only one who moved from faithful doubting to passionate love could so willingly offer his all.

Southern writer Flannery O'Connor has taught me something that has made me healthier as a Christian. I think it will make you healthier too. She says that the cultivation of skepticism is a sacred obligation because skepticism will keep you free—not free to do anything you please, but free to be formed by something larger than your own intellect or the intellects of those around you.[7]

The disciple Thomas, to his credit, refused to say that he understood what he did not understand—or that he believed what he did not believe. There was an uncompromising honesty about him that is to be admired. He refused to deny his doubts—and we should too:

> My Lord God, I have no idea where I am going. I do not see the road ahead of me. I cannot know for sure where it will end. Nor do I really know myself, and the fact that

---

7. Dark, *The Sacredness of Questioning Everything*, 31.

Doubt

I think I'm following your will does not mean that I am actually doing so. But I believe that the desire to please you does in fact please you. And I hope I have that desire in all that I am doing. I hope that I will never do anything apart from that desire. And I know that, if I do this, you will lead me by the right road, though I may know nothing about it. Therefore, I will trust you always though I may seem to be lost and in the shadow of death. I will not fear, for you are ever with me, and you will never leave me to face my perils alone.[8]

---

8. Merton, *Raids on the Unspeakable*, 72–73.

8

Miracles

As Peter traveled about the country, he went to visit the Lord's people who lived in Lydda. There he found a man named Aeneas, who was paralyzed and had been bedridden for eight years. "Aeneas," Peter said to him, "Jesus Christ heals you. Get up and roll up your mat." Immediately Aeneas got up. All those who lived in Lydda and Sharon saw him and turned to the Lord. In Joppa there was a disciple named Tabitha (in Greek her name is Dorcas); she was always doing good and helping the poor. About that time, she became sick and died, and her body was washed and placed in an upstairs room. Lydda was near Joppa; so, when the disciples heard that Peter was in Lydda, they sent two men to him and urged him, "Please come at once!" Peter went with them, and when he arrived, he was taken upstairs to the room. All the widows stood around him, crying and showing him the robes and other clothing that Dorcas had made while she was still with them. Peter sent them all out of the room; then he got down on his knees and prayed. Turning toward the dead woman, he said, "Tabitha, get up." She opened her eyes and seeing Peter she sat up. He took her by the hand

Miracles

and helped her to her feet. Then he called for the believers, especially the widows, and presented her to them alive. This became known all over Joppa, and many people believed in the Lord. Peter stayed in Joppa for some time with a tanner named Simon.

—Acts 9:32–43

We modern people think of miracles as the suspension of the natural order. The Bible tells us that God did not originally make the world to have disease, hunger, and death in it. Jesus has come to redeem where it is wrong and heal the world where it is broken. His miracles are not just proofs that he has power but also wonderful foretastes of what he is going to do with that power. Jesus's miracles are not just a challenge to our minds, but a promise to our hearts, that the world we all want is coming.

—Tim Keller

Have you ever wondered why God chooses to heal some but not others? In 1997, I attended a conference in California and heard John Wimber, founder of the Vineyard Movement, giving his testimony. Wimber wrote several best-selling books about miracles and healing. What he taught was called "Power Evangelism," the belief that the preaching of the gospel should be accompanied by the signs and wonders of healing and deliverance.

At the end of his sermon that day, he invited people to come forward for prayer. He said, "We are going to call out several symptoms. If any of these symptoms describe you, please come forward and tell us." I have always been skeptical of faith healing, but that week, I was listening with different ears. You see, two days earlier, my doctor had found a growth in my right sinus. I was scheduled

Miracles

for surgery two weeks later to determine if the growth was malignant. I said to myself, "God, I want to believe this. If there's anything to this, let him describe my symptoms."

I sat there listening to every kind of ailment being mentioned, including heart problems, arthritis, and back pain, and then I heard the words I'll never forget: "There is someone here who has been told this week that they have a growth in their right sinus." I could not believe what I was hearing. Something moved me out of my chair, and I went forward.

A young man about my son's age came to me and said, "Do you mind if I lay my hand on your chest?"

"No, I don't mind, go ahead," I said. What happened next is incredible.

This young man told me that the Holy Spirit was revealing that the growth was benign, that I would be fine, and that I could quit worrying. "Also," he said, "the Holy Spirit says you should rest more." I knew then that what he said came straight from God. Two weeks later, I had the surgery, and as this young man had prophesied, the growth was benign.

John Wimber taught me much that day about being open to the miraculous. He also taught me something else. He taught me that miracles sometimes come in ways we do not expect. He died later that year, having suffered greatly over the four previous years with a heart attack, a stroke, and finally cancer. After being diagnosed with an inoperable tumor, he wrote an article called "Signs, Wonders, and Cancer." He ended the article with these words:

> While I was being treated for cancer, someone wrote me a letter asking, "Do you still believe in healing now that you've got cancer?" I wrote back: "Yes! I do." And the truth is, I do.
>
> I also believe in pain. Both are found in the Word of God. In the year I spent battling cancer, God purged me of a lot of habits and attitudes that weren't right, and through it I grew stronger as a Christian. Some of my greatest spiritual advances in spiritual maturity came as I embraced the pain—as each day I had to choose to allow

Miracles

> God to accomplish his work in me by any method, even adversity . . .
>
> Going through the valley of the shadow is frightening. Its uncertainties keep you alert to every changing scenario. I began to cling to every nuance of the doctor's words, shrugs, and grimaces. I experienced the full range of emotions that go with life-threatening illness. I wept as I saw my utter need to depend on God . . . I had to embrace the truth that I could not control my life . . . I also found that the view from the valley gave me a focus on Christ that I would not have found any other way.[1]

When John Wimber became a Christian back in the 1960s, he came to faith as part of the Jesus Movement in Southern California. Without any church background whatsoever, God transformed Wimber's life incredibly:

> One Sunday he wandered into a church and after the service he approached the pastor and said, "Hey, your sermon really made me think and the music was great. But when do we get to the cool stuff?" The pastor looked puzzled and asked, "The cool stuff?" Wimber replied, "Yeh, the cool stuff. You know, like healing people and raising them from the dead. The cool stuff I've been reading about in the New Testament." The pastor thought for a moment and then said, "I'm sorry, we don't do the cool stuff here. You might try another church down the street, but I doubt they're doing the cool stuff you're talking about either."[2]

Why is it that the modern church no longer does the "cool stuff" as Wimber called it in his early days as a Christian? When have you ever witnessed anything like what Peter did in Lydda and Joppa?

> As Peter traveled about the country, he went to visit the Lord's people who lived in Lydda. There he found a man named Aeneas, who was paralyzed and had been bedridden for eight years. "Aeneas," Peter said to him, "Jesus

---

1. Wimber, "Signs, Wonders, and Cancer," 49–50.
2. Wimber, "When Do We Get to do the Good Stuff?".

Miracles

Christ heals you. Get up and roll up your mat." Immediately, Aeneas got up (Acts 9:32–34).

In Joppa there was a disciple named Tabitha (in Greek her name was Dorcas); she was always doing good and helping the poor. About that time she became sick and died, and her body was washed and placed in an upstairs room. Lydda was near Joppa; so when the disciples heard that Peter was in Lydda, they sent two men to him and urged him, "Please come at once." Peter went with them, and when he arrived he was taken upstairs to the room. All the widows stood around him, crying and showing him the robes and other clothing that Dorcas had made while she was still with them. Peter sent them all out of the room; then he got down on his knees and prayed. Turning toward the dead woman, he said, "Tabitha, get up." She opened her eyes, and seeing Peter she sat up. He took her by the hand and helped her to her feet. Then he called for the believers, especially the widows, and presented her to them alive (Acts 9:36–41).

There are still a lot of John Wimbers in the world, and they are wondering why we do not see these kinds of miracles anymore.

Interestingly, in scripture, God usually reserves these kinds of miracles for brief, remarkable periods of time—just prior to his making a big change in how he interacts with his creation. In fact, most miracles, though certainly not all miracles in the Bible, are limited to three relatively short, extremely exceptional periods in biblical history:

1. The Exodus, wanderings, and conquest. After four hundred years of silence, God astonished the Egyptians and Hebrews with a series of miraculous events as he freed his covenant people from slavery in Egypt and then settled them in the Promised Land.

2. The Prophetic Ministries of Elijah and Elisha. In the days of the kings, after many decades of warnings, God sent these two prophets to turn Israel from idolatry. He then used miracles to validate their message as divine.

Miracles

3. The Foundational Ministries of Christ and the apostles. After four hundred years of silence, God sent his Son with the ability to accomplish miraculous feats that rivaled the miraculous periods of the Old Testament. He then produced miracles through the apostles to validate the message of Jesus Christ as heaven-sent.[3]

Although miracles are rare in scripture, God has always been at work in the world supernaturally. And there is a difference in the supernatural and the miraculous. When God created all things, he devised the laws of nature, such as gravity and thermodynamics, to give order to everything in the universe. Most of the time, God allows the cosmos to work according to the laws of nature, and when he takes steps to advance his plan, he usually works through the laws of nature and not against them.

My favorite Bible character is Joseph, son of Jacob. Do you know there are no recorded miracles in either of their stories? Joseph explains how his brothers' evil act of selling him into slavery was used by God to do great good:

> You intended to harm me, but God intended it for good
> to accomplish what is now being done, the saving of
> many lives (Genesis 50:20).

Notice how Joseph says what his brothers did was evil. They intended harm, and it was deliberate, yet God intervened and used Joseph's troubles and sorrows for his own good purposes.

Jacob, Joseph's father, deceived his father and brother. As a result, he had to flee his homeland and experience great suffering and injustice. Far from home, he met the love of his life and had his children through whom Jesus is descended. Jacob's sin did not lead to plan B of God's will for his life. There is no plan B.

Jacob was responsible for his sin, and he had to suffer for his foolish choices, but God was infallibly in control, working supernaturally in all sorts of ways. God creates what appear to be coincidental circumstances that empower people to accomplish what they otherwise could not. These are supernatural activities in

---

3. Swindoll, *Swindoll's Living Insights*, 180–89.

Miracles

contrast to miracles like healing the sick and raising the dead. Miracles occur to validate an event or to make an undeniable display of divine power to draw everyone's attention and to authenticate the activity or message as unmistakably God's:

- He parts the waters of the sea.
- He causes a donkey to speak.
- He causes an ax-head to float.
- He allows three young men to be cast into a blazing fire, and they all emerge without a hair being singed.

These are authentic miracles in which God contravenes the laws of nature for his purposes. However, they are rare. Even though miracles are few and far between, God never ceases to work supernaturally (beyond human comprehension).

In a sermon about Jesus feeding the five thousand, pastor and writer Nadia Bolz Weber beautifully articulates our need to believe God can do more:

> I've read many rational explanations for what really happened at the feeding of the five thousand. Explanations you could offer to your non-churchy friends without feeling like you have to apologize for being so silly as to believe in real miracles. With very little effort we can easily explain away the feeding of the five thousand as little more than . . . a wilderness potluck where everybody felt so compelled to be good people after hearing Jesus preach that they opened up their picnic baskets and gave parts of their fried chicken and potato salad to their neighbors.
>
> But I just couldn't bear to preach a "Jesus wants you to be nice and share your lunchbox" sermon today. Because miracles, and not lessons about sharing, are what we really need. So as crazy as it is, I believe in miracles—not because I think I'm supposed to, but because I need to. I need to believe God does what we cannot do. If human reason were enough to love and save and create beautiful

Miracles

things out of dust, then Christ died in vain and the promise is null. No brothers and sisters, I want some miracles.[4]

I too want some miracles, believing God does what we cannot do. When I am tempted to rely on what I can do, I forget about Jesus, the one who is continually making something out of my nothing, multiplying my little into his much. Jesus always does more.

Our suffering is bearable when we come to believe there is always more, when we know deep down that life is not meaningless but purposeful, part of the Storyteller's infinite imagination. In this life, we will never fully know why God heals some and not others. The answer will be given at the end of the story, and all who hear it and see its fulfillment will find it completely satisfying and infinitely sufficient.

I do not think anyone has surpassed Dostoevsky's summation in *The Brothers Karamazov* as to how things will end:

> I believe like a child that suffering will be healed and made up for, that all the humiliating absurdity of human contradictions will vanish like a pitiful mirage, like the despicable fabrication of the impotent and infinitely small Euclidean mind of man, that in the world's finale, at the moment of eternal harmony, something so precious will come to pass that it will suffice for all hearts, for the comforting of all resentments, for the atonement of all crimes of humanity, of all the blood they have shed; that it will make it not only possible to forgive but to justify all that has happened.[5]

Our relationship with Jesus Christ offers a consolation and a restoration of the life we have and the life we have always wanted and never achieved.

It takes faith to believe in this kind of miracle, a deep abiding radical trust in the goodness of God. I will never doubt that a good God is telling a good story that will have a good ending. I believe as Job did:

4. Bolz Weber, "Sermon on the Feeding of the 5000."
5. Dostoevsky, *The Brothers Karamazov*, 235–36.

Miracles

Though he slay me, yet will I hope in him (Job 13:15).

Habakkuk's declaration is mine as well:

> Though the fig tree does not bud and there are no grapes on the vines, though the olive crop fails and the fields produce no food, though there are no sheep in the pen and no cattle in the stalls, yet will I rejoice in the Lord, I will be joyful in God my Savior (Habakkuk 3:17–18).

Radical trust is the result of unswerving belief in a God of miracles.

9

Discouragement

Listen to my words, Lord, consider my lament. Hear my cry for help, my King and my God, for to you I pray. In the morning, Lord, you hear my voice; in the morning I lay my requests before you and wait expectantly. For you are not a God who is pleased with wickedness; with you, evil people are not welcome. The arrogant cannot stand in your presence. You hate all who do wrong; you destroy those who tell lies. The bloodthirsty and deceitful you, Lord, detest. But I, by your great love, can come into your house; in reverence I bow down toward your holy temple. Lead me, Lord, in your righteousness because of my enemies—make your way straight before me. Not a word from their mouth can be trusted; their heart is filled with malice. Their throat is an open grave; with their tongues they tell lies. Declare them guilty, O God! Let their intrigues be their downfall. Banish them for their many sins, for they have rebelled against you. But let all who take refuge in you be glad; let them ever sing for joy. Spread your protection over them, that those who love your name may rejoice in you. Surely,

Discouragement

Lord, you bless the righteous; you surround them with your favor as with a shield.

—Psalm 5:1–12

In time of dryness and desolation, we must be patient, and wait with resignation the return of consolation, putting our trust in the goodness of God. We must animate ourselves by the thought that God is always with us, that he only allows this trial for our greater good, and that we have not necessarily lost his grace because we have lost the taste and feeling of it.

—Ignatius of Loyola

For those who use the King James Version of the Bible, you will notice that David, the author of this psalm, this song, wanted it played on an instrument called a Nehiloth, an ancient woodwind instrument similar to the flute. It seems many of the lament psalms were played on this instrument.

We know from scripture that David played the lyre, an instrument like today's harp:

> Whenever the spirit from God came on Saul, David would take up his lyre and play. Then relief would come to Saul; he would feel better, and the evil spirit would leave him (1 Samuel 16:23).

It appears David himself did not play the Nehiloth, but perhaps preferred the timbre of its sounds to express his own moods of discouragement and sadness.

David, in Psalm 5, is discouraged, and we can imagine it was the result of an atmosphere of strife and opposition of some sort. David is down and discouraged, and that lends understanding to why he would compose this ancient hymn in a minor key. Maybe

Discouragement

this could be the kind of music that best describes the situation or atmosphere you find yourself in from time to time.

Discouragement can be a deep, dark hole, and we have all been there, haven't we?

- some project or dream has failed
- some relationship has gone south
- we are physically or mentally exhausted
- our health is not what it used to be
- we do not have money to meet our needs

In Psalm 5, David is in an emotional slump, and Eugene Peterson's paraphrase helps us, even more, to place ourselves in David's shoes:

> Listen, God! Please, pay attention!
> Can you make sense of these ramblings,
> my groans and cries?
> King-God, I need your help.
> Every morning
> you'll hear me at it again.
> Every morning
> I lay out the pieces of my life
> on your altar
> and watch for fire to descend.
> You don't socialize with Wicked,
> or invite Evil over as your houseguest.
> Hot-Air-Boaster collapses in front of you;
> you shake your head over Mischief-Maker.
> God destroys Lie-Speaker;
> Blood-Thirsty and Truth-Bender disgust you.
> And here I am, your invited guest—
> it's incredible!
> I enter your house; here I am,
> prostrate in your inner sanctum,
> Waiting for directions
> to get me safely through enemy lines.
> Every word they speak is a land mine;
> their lungs breathe out poison gas.

Discouragement

> Their throats are gaping graves,
> their tongues slick as mudslides.
> Pile on the guilt, God!
> Let their so-called wisdom wreck them.
> Kick them out! They've had their chance.
> But you'll welcome us with open arms
> when we run for cover to you.
> Let the party last all night!
> Stand guard over our celebration.
> You are famous, God, for welcoming God-seekers,
> for decking us out in delight
> (Psalm 5:1–12, *The Message*).

Notice carefully when reading Psalm 5 that after David lists his lament in verses 1–3, he begins to say certain things about God in verses 4–6:

- You are not a God who takes pleasure in wickedness.
- No evil dwells in you.
- The boastful cannot stand before your eyes.
- You hate those who do iniquity.
- You destroy those who speak falsely.
- You abhor those who shed blood and spread deceit.

Do you see what David is doing? He is reviewing the attributes of God, and in doing so, he is reminding himself that God is *for* him and not against him. David has discovered for himself and is teaching us that focusing on God helps dispel discouragement. It is therapeutic.

Sometimes when we find ourselves so discouraged that it is difficult to count our blessings, we need to begin counting the attributes of God. I do not know what your prayer life is like. Perhaps you are bored stiff with the way you are praying. If you are anything like me, you are probably praying the same prayer, or type of prayer, day after day.

Why don't we take a page out of David's playbook, David's prayer book, David's hymnal, and begin praying the attributes of

Discouragement

God? This could make all the difference in the world and give us a whole new way of facing our problems and rallying our weary souls.

As I have exceeded threescore and ten, I have come to recognize that there are three attributes of God that I turn to most when I am discouraged:

- the goodness of God
- the power of God
- the providence of God

Focusing on these three attributes, I, like David, can encourage myself and weather any storm that comes my way. You can do the same.

First, let us consider the goodness of God. A. W. Tozer says, "What comes to our mind when we think about God is the most important thing about us."[1] The greater our view of God, the more strength we will have to face the trials of life.

There was a time in the life of Moses when he needed the assurance of God's presence. The burden seemed too much for one man to shoulder:

> Moses said to the Lord, "You have been telling me, 'Lead these people,' but you have not let me know whom you will send with me. You have said, 'I know you by name and you have found favor with me.' If you are pleased with me, teach me your ways so I may know you and continue to find favor with you. Remember that this nation is your people." The Lord replied, "My Presence will go with you, and I will give you rest." Then Moses said to him, "If your Presence does not go with us, do not send us up from here. How will anyone know that you are pleased with me and with your people unless you go with us? What else will distinguish me and your people from all the other people on the face of the earth?" And the Lord said to Moses, "I will do the very thing you have asked, because I am pleased with you and I know you

---

1. Tozer, *The Knowledge of the Holy*, 1.

Discouragement

> by name." Then Moses said, "Now show me your glory."
> And the Lord said, "I will cause all my goodness to pass in front of you, and I will proclaim my name, the Lord, in your presence. I will have mercy on whom I will have mercy, and I will have compassion on whom I will have compassion. But," he said, "you cannot see my face, for no one may see me and live." Then the Lord said, "There is a place near me where you may stand on a rock. When my glory passes by, I will put you in a cleft in the rock and cover you with my hand until I have passed by. Then I will remove my hand and you will see my back; but my face must not be seen" (Exodus 33:12–23).

Do not miss what is being said here. God covered Moses in the cleft of the rock and allowed him to see just the backside of his goodness, and that was enough to make his face glow. Like Moses, if we could just see the backside of God's goodness, our faces would glow as well.

There is one thing I will never doubt: a good God is telling a good story that will have a good ending. In scripture, the word *good* is used more to describe God than the word *love*:

> Taste and see that the Lord is good; blessed are those who take refuge in him (Psalm 34:8).

> Give thanks to the Lord for he is good (1 Chronicles 16:34).

> The Lord is good, a refuge in times of trouble (Nahum 1:7).

Are you seeing the protection offered when we accentuate the attribute of God's goodness? Refuge and stronghold are the words used.

Our dictionaries are way too small. Our definition of *good* is far too weak. We need to follow David's example, taking our eyes off our problems in order to refocus our attention on the attributes of God—attributes like his goodness:

Discouragement

> For the Lord is good and his love endures forever; his faithfulness continues through all generations (Psalm 100:5).

We think about God's goodness when times are tough, and we should. At the same time, we should remember that God is omnipotent (all-powerful). Being omnipotent God can do anything that he chooses to do. An even simpler definition would be *God is able.*

Rabbi Harold Kushner, author of the international best-seller *When Bad Things Happen to Good People*, watched his child die at a young age from a rare disease that caused his body to age rapidly. Working through his pain and grief theologically, Rabbi Kushner came to the only conclusion that could satisfy him. Very simply, he concluded that God is not omnipotent. There are events beyond God's control.

Rabbi Kushner's dilemma was that he could not harmonize God's goodness and God's omnipotence. If God were truly good and all-powerful, he would never have allowed the death of Kushner's son, the Holocaust, earthquakes, or tornados. Kushner gave up one attribute (omnipotence) to cling to another (goodness). For Kushner, you cannot have both—only one—and he opted for God's goodness. He ends his book this way:

> Are you capable of forgiving and loving God even when you have found out he is not perfect, even when he has let you down and disappointed you by permitting bad luck and sickness and cruelty in his world, and permitting some of those things to happen to you? Can you learn to love and forgive him despite his limitations, as Job does, and as you once learned to forgive and love your parents even though they were not as wise, as strong, or as perfect as you needed them to be?[2]

I am sure you caught Kushner's two most important declarations: God is not perfect, and God has limitations. God is good, but he is not omnipotent. As a Christian, I believe otherwise. I

---

2. Kushner, *When Bad Things Happen to Good People*, 162.

Discouragement

believe God is good and he *desires* the best for us. I also believe God is omniscient (all-knowing) and he *knows* what is best for us. And, unlike Rabbi Kushner, I believe God is omnipotent (all-powerful) and is *able* to bring about what is best for us.

For me, there is one verse that settles the question once and for all. It's what our Lord Jesus said in the Garden of Gethsemane hours before he would be nailed to the cross:

> "*Abba*, Father," he said, "everything is possible for you. Take this cup from me. Yet, not what I will, but what you will" (Mark 14:36).

As a parent who has also buried a child, I can say Rabbi Kushner's conclusion—that God is not omnipotent—gives me no comfort at all. In fact, his own wife is on record as saying she derived no comfort from her husband's conclusions. Believing in God's omnipotence gives me hope that no power in all creation can stop God or hinder his plans. Not evil men, not natural catastrophe, not reversal of fortune, not fate, not luck, not chance, not human error, not even Satan himself.

Martin Luther said, "The devil is God's devil and will serve God's purposes."

> For the message of the cross is foolishness to those who are perishing, but to us who are being saved it is the power of God (1 Corinthians 1:18).

To the natural mind, the cross was a terrible waste, a tragedy, an enormous mistake. But to the spiritually enlightened, it is a demonstration of the power of God. In the very place God seems defeated, we see his power. If God were not omnipotent, Jesus would still be dead. God can raise the dead because he can do anything.

Although I had to bury my child, I know God has the power to raise her up, and I know that he will some glorious day. Like David in Psalm 5, I encourage myself by praying the attributes of God: goodness, omnipotence, and providence. Oliver Wendell Holmes said, "The great act of faith is when a man decides he is not God." That is what I have come to believe. I gave up long ago trying

Discouragement

to be the god of my own life. I let go of the reins and surrendered my life to the God and Father of our Lord Jesus Christ.

I have given God control. I trust him, and I have faith that I am secure in him and that he will take care of me for all eternity. I do not have to be anxious or worry because I know he is in complete control of all things. I know he will complete his plan for my life. Being secure is not the same as being safe. We are never safe in a fallen world, but we are eternally secure.

Another scripture that has kept me upright and stable and on course is Proverbs 3:5–6:

> Trust in the Lord with all your heart and lean not on your own understanding; in all your ways submit to him, and he will make your paths straight.

I remember reading about the prevenient grace of God as a young seminary student—the grace that goes before. It is the belief that in every situation of life, God is already at work before we get there. God is working creatively, strategically, and redemptively for our good and his glory.

How often do we limit our thinking to the fact that God's presence goes with us as we journey through life? That is certainly the case, but it is only part of our story. God is with us now, and he is already way up the road ahead of us. While we are struggling with today's problems, God is at work providing for the things we will face tomorrow. Imagine that! God is already ahead of us, already there, working creatively in situations we have yet to face, preparing them for us and us for them.

I remember receiving a book in the mail many years ago when we were young missionaries in Brazil. *An Overwhelming Interference* by Edward Kuhlman is the touching story of how a heartbroken, grieving father faced the death of his beloved son (Kuhlman 1986). The book moved me deeply and I thought, *this will help me in my ministry to assist those who have to face such a terrible tragedy*. Little did I know God was preparing me for my own tragedy, the saddest day of my life—the day my youngest child, Leigh Alexandra, died suddenly, without warning, with an occult heart ailment called myocarditis. I have now had nearly three decades to process and grieve her death, and I am as certain today as I was before her death that a good God is telling a good story that will have a good ending. Good for Edward Kuhlman and his son, good for Alexandra and our family, and good for you, the person reading these words.

In facing difficult days when we find it hard even to pray, let's remember something I heard that Bono (a Christian), U2's lead singer, does on the nights he doesn't have the voice to hit the high notes. When time for the high notes comes, he turns the mic toward the audience and lets the crowd sing. The crowd does for him that he cannot do for himself: sing. Perhaps we should do the same and follow Bono's lead. When we have no voice to hit the high notes, we can turn to the great cloud of witnesses and let them sing for us:

> Therefore, since we are surrounded by such a great cloud of witnesses, let us throw off everything that hinders and the sin that so easily entangles. And let us run with perseverance the race marked out for us (Hebrews 12:1).

10

Unique

Do not let your hearts be troubled. Trust in God; trust also in me. My Father's house has plenty of room; if that were not so, would I have told you that I am going there to prepare a place for you? And if I go and prepare a place for you, I will come back and take you to be with me that you also may be where I am. You know the way to the place where I am going. Thomas said to him, "Lord, we don't know where you are going, so how can we know the way?" Jesus answered, "I am the way and the truth and the life. No one comes to the Father except through me. If you really know me, you will know my Father as well. From now on, you do know him and have seen him.

—John 14:1–7

The Word we study has to be the Word we pray. My personal experience of the relentless tenderness of God came not from exegetes, theologians, and spiritual writers, but from sitting still in the presence of the living Word and beseeching

Unique

him to help me understand with my head and heart his written Word. Sheer scholarship alone cannot reveal to us the gospel of grace. We must never allow the authority of books, institutions, or leaders to replace the authority of knowing Jesus Christ personally and directly. When the religious views of others interpose between us and the primary experience of Jesus as the Christ, we become unconvicted and unpersuasive travel agents handing out brochures to places we have never visited.

—Brennan Manning

A few years ago, Fox News commentator Brit Hume made a comment about Tiger Woods, whose marriage was coming to an end because of multiple adulterous affairs. Hume said that Tiger could possibly save his golfing career but salvaging his personal life would be another matter. Hume reasoned that since Tiger is a Buddhist, and in Buddhism, there is not the kind of forgiveness and redemption offered by the Christian faith, that he could turn to Christ, make a total recovery, and be a tremendous testimony to the world.

As you would guess, Brit Hume's comments met with an avalanche of criticism. He was labeled ignorant, corrupt, inept, morally bankrupt, and things appearing on YouTube too vulgar to put into print.

What Brit Hume said about Buddhism is correct. Whatever its virtues, Buddhism does not offer the kind of forgiveness and redemption that are central to the Christian faith. Perhaps the major difference between Christianity and Buddhism is that Buddhism does not promote belief in God—if God is defined as a personal being who created the universe by design.

Pay close attention to what Brit Hume said. He did not say that Buddhism does not teach virtues (it does), or that there are few good things about it (there are many). But forgiveness and

Unique

redemption are not cornerstones of Buddhism as they are in Christianity. The intensity of offense taken at Hume's remarks is revealing. The uniqueness of Jesus as taught by Christians has always been a stumbling block to those who believe no one religion contains all truth.

Jesus believed himself to be unique and the only way to personal relationship with God. Scripture makes this undeniably clear:

> All things have been committed to me by my Father. No one knows the Son except the Father, and no one knows the Father except the Son and those to whom the Son chooses to reveal him. Come to me, all you who are weary and burdened, and I will give you rest (Matthew 11:27-28).

> Then they asked him, "What must we do to do the works God requires?" Jesus answered, "The work of God is this: to believe in the one he has sent" (John 6:28-29).

> I am the bread of life. Whoever comes to me will never go hungry, and whoever believes in me will never be thirsty...For my Father's will is that everyone who looks to the Son and believes in him shall have eternal life, and I will raise them up at the last day (John 6:35, 40).

> I am the light of the world. Whoever follows me will never walk in darkness but, will have the light of life (John 8:12).

> I am the resurrection and the life. Anyone who believes in me will live, even though they die; and whoever lives by believing in me will never die (John 11:25-26).

> I am the way and the truth and the life. No one comes to the Father except through me. If you really know me, you will know my Father as well (John 14:6-7a).

Postmodernists have difficulty with the claims of Jesus. They are quick to accept Jesus as a great moral teacher, but they reject his claims to be the unique Son of God. C. S. Lewis responds:

Unique

> That is the one thing we must not say. A man who was merely a man and said the sort of things Jesus said would not be a great moral teacher. He would be either a lunatic—on a level with the man who says he is a poached egg—or else he would be the devil of hell. You must make your choice. Either this man was, and is, the Son of God: or else a madman or something worse. You can shut him up for a fool, you can spit at him and kill him as a demon; or you can fall at his feet and call him Lord and God.[1]

When Jesus was involved in a dispute about the Sabbath, he claimed to be Lord of the Sabbath (Mark 2:23–27). In another argument about the Sabbath, Jesus said, "My Father is always at work to this very day, and I, too, am working" (John 5:17). For this reason, they tried all the more to kill him; not only was he breaking the Sabbath, but he was even calling God his own Father, making himself equal with God (John 5:18). Notice that Jesus did not oppose their conclusions. Jesus ended another dispute by saying, "Before Abraham was, I am" (John 8:58). Hearing this, the Jews sought to stone him because he was claiming to have existed "as God" before he was born in Bethlehem.

You may think that all religions are equal, but they are not. Jesus's claim to be God in flesh makes him unique. Buddha claimed no such thing. Neither did Muhammad nor Confucius.

After his resurrection, Jesus appeared to his disciple Thomas, who had doubted his master was raised from the dead. When Thomas met the risen Lord, he cried out, "My Lord, and my God" (John 20:28). Jesus accepted Thomas's worship.

The book of Revelation tells us that a host of angels and saints are continually worshipping "the Lamb who was slain" (Revelation 5:12–13). No other religious leader in history is accorded this honor because none other deserves it. What other religious leader claimed to die for the sin of humanity? Jesus said, "The Son of Man came to seek and to save what was lost" (Luke 19:10), and "to give his life a ransom for many" (Matthew 20:28). Many have claimed

---

1. Lewis, *Mere Christianity*, 52.

Unique

to know the way to God, but none have claimed to be the one and only way to God.

Now if we are not careful, we will misunderstand what Jesus is saying about himself. This is where Brit Hume could have been clearer in his comments. Jesus did not say that the religion we call Christianity is the only way to God. He said *he* was the only way.

Christianity as a religion is humanly flawed. Look at the hundreds of pedophile priests in the Catholic Church and Protestant ministers doing exactly what Tiger Woods did and worse. Sadly, Christianity, like all religions, is subject to error and corruption. Jesus is not a Christian. For that, you can be glad. Christians and Christianity will fall short, but Jesus never will. He will always be the way, the truth, and the life.

Christians need to understand that Jesus never implied that there is no truth in other religions. My own faith as a Baptist minister has been enriched by certain truths I have found in the writings of other religions, including Judaism, Zen Buddhism, and Native American spirituality, just to name three.

Jesus had many interactions with those of other faith traditions, such as the Roman centurion who had a sick servant (Luke 7); the Canaanite woman whose daughter was sick (Matthew 15); the Samaritan leper, grateful for his healing (Luke 17); the Samaritan woman at the well (John 4); and the unnamed sick and demonized from the regions of Syria and Decapolis who were not Jewish. In each case, Jesus healed the sick, delivered those oppressed by demons, told them to share what God had done for them, and praised them for their great faith. He did not follow Jewish prejudicial norms, condemn or rebuke, warn of judgment or hell, or argue theology and debate scripture. *He* was all they truly needed.

We are not called to condemn other religions, and in no way was Brit Hume condemning Buddhism in his comments about Tiger Woods. He merely pointed out that Christianity, in its teaching about Jesus, offers something Buddhism does not: forgiveness and redemption through Jesus Christ. Jesus Christ is the standard by which we judge all religions, including our own.

Unique

Christianity should never be defined by its boundaries but by its center. Moral codes, religious activities, and denominational distinctions are boundary markers often used to separate and exclude, but the center of the Christian faith is a person—and to be Christian is to know this person. Sadly, Christianity will not always look like Jesus.

Tony Campolo, a sociologist and preacher from Eastern University in Philadelphia, was at a conference in Hawaii. Unable to sleep because of the time change, at 3:30 a.m., he went out and found an open diner to grab a bite to eat. As he sat there eating, a group of prostitutes walked in and sat near where he was seated. It was easy to hear their conversation, and one of the women said, "Tomorrow is my birthday, and you know I've never had a birthday party!"

After the group left, Campolo asked the owner, a man named Harry, if the woman having a birthday came there often.

"Oh yes, they come here every night," said Harry. "Her name is Agnes."

"Would you help me throw her a party with a cake tomorrow night?" Campolo asked.

"Of course! I would be glad to," said Harry.

When Agnes and her friends arrived the next evening, Campolo, Harry, and all the employees yelled, "Surprise!"

As they sang "Happy Birthday," Agnes burst into tears. When it came time to cut the cake, Agnes made an interesting request. She asked if she could take the cake quickly to show her mother and that she would return shortly. While Agnes was gone, Tony Campolo asked everyone if they would take a moment and join him in praying for Agnes. When he said, "Amen," Harry leaned over and said, "You never said you were a preacher. What kind of preacher are you—and what kind of church do you attend?"

Tony Campolo just grinned and said, "I belong to the kind of church that throws birthday parties for prostitutes at three thirty in the morning."

Harry replied, "No, you don't; if there were a church like that, I'd join it."[2]

No religion can do that—only Jesus can. Christianity, at its best, always reflects the good news that we are loved, we are accepted, and we are who God says we are: the beloved for whom Christ died. His sacrifice will always be better than our religiosity. Our sins may be great, but Jesus is greater. He is more than our worst and best moments.

---

2. Campolo, *The Kingdom of God Is a Party*, 4–8.

11

Grace

For the kingdom of heaven is like a landowner who went out early in the morning to hire workers for his vineyard. He agreed to pay them a denarius for the day and sent them into his vineyard. About nine in the morning he went out and saw others standing in the marketplace doing nothing. He told them, "You also go and work in my vineyard, and I will pay you whatever is right." So they went. He went out again about noon and about three in the afternoon and did the same thing. About five in the afternoon he went out and found still others standing around. He asked them, "Why have you been standing here all day long doing nothing?" "Because no one has hired us," they answered. He said to them, "You also go and work in my vineyard." When evening came, the owner of the vineyard said to his supervisor, "Call the workers and pay them their wages, beginning with the last ones hired and going on to the first." The workers who were hired about five in the afternoon came and each received a denarius. So when those came who were hired first, they expected to receive more. But each one of them also received a denarius. When they received it, they began

Grace

to grumble against the landowner. "These who were hired last worked only one hour," they said, "and you have made them equal to us who have borne the burden of the work and the heat of the day." But he answered one of them, "I am not being unfair to you, friend. Didn't you agree to work for a denarius? Take your pay and go. I want to give the one who was hired last the same as I gave you. Don't I have the right to do what I want with my own money? Or are you envious because I am generous?" So the last will be first, and the first will be last.

—Matthew 20:1–16

Grace is the celebration of life, relentlessly hounding all the non-celebrants in the world. It is a floating, cosmic bash shouting its way through the streets of the universe, flinging the sweetness of its cassations to every window, pounding at every door in a hilarity beyond all liking and happening, until the prodigals come out at last and dance, and the elder brothers finally take their fingers out of their ears.

—Robert Farrar Capon

As a young minister, I believed the Bible was the most important thing in my life, the ultimate source of authority. It pointed me to Jesus. Over the years, I came to believe that my ultimate allegiance belongs not to the Bible but to the one of whom the Bible testifies: Jesus Christ.

I spent my early years as a young pastor wishing God could be more like Jesus. But now, I have no doubt whatsoever. God is like Jesus. In fact, if I am honest, I have never known a God of wrath. The God I have experienced is the God of Jesus, the God almost too good to be described. A God of unconditional love. A

God who brought us into being in an explosion of creative love. A God who longs for us more than we long for him. A God who does not want us to fear him but to love him. Scripture is clear. "There is no fear in love. But perfect love drives out fear, because fear has to do with punishment. The one who fears is not made perfect in love" (1 John 4:18).

We become like the God we worship. That is why the first of the Ten Commandments is "You shall have no other gods before me" (Exodus 20:3). When we believe in a God of love, we begin to love. Jesus taught the primacy of love in both word and deed:

> Love the Lord your God with all your heart and with all your soul and with all your strength and with all your mind, and, love your neighbor as yourself (Luke 10:27).

If God is as good and loving as Jesus says he is, then we can live and love and give and forgive in ways we've never imagined.

Jesus did not give us the parable of the vineyard workers just to teach us how to live. He gave us the parable to correct our notion of how and who God loves. It is a perplexing parable because it is easy for us to identify with the offended workers who had labored from sunrise to sunset only to watch, in amazement, as the slackers receive the very same all-day salary.

Can't you imagine the hooting and hollering that went on when one-hour workers received their pay? It is important to note that the landowner paid those who came to work last—*first*! He paid those who labored all day—*last*! Jesus tells the story this way to upset our notion of fairness. It was not fair—but thank goodness God is not fair. What if God did deal with us precisely the way we deserve?

In *What's So Amazing About Grace?* Philip Yancey summarized why we should be extremely grateful that God is a God of mercy and not simply the God of justice:

> Jesus's story makes no economic sense, and that was his intent. He has given us a parable about grace, which cannot be calculated like a day's wages. The employer in Jesus's story did not cheat the full-day workers. No, the full-day workers got what they were promised. Their discontent arose from the scandalous mathematics of grace.

> They would not accept that their employer had the right to do what he wanted with his money when it meant paying scoundrels twelve times what they deserved. Significantly, many Christians who study this parable identify with the employees who put in a full day's work, rather than the add-ons at the end of the day. We like to think of ourselves as responsible workers, and the employer's strange behavior baffles us as it did the original hearers. We risk missing the point: that God dispenses gifts, not wages. None of us gets paid according to merit, for none of us comes close to satisfying God's requirements for a perfect life. If paid on the basis of fairness, we would all end up in hell.[1]

If God kept strict accounts, we would be growing deeper in debt every day. But God's grace, love, and mercy are extended equally to everyone, absolutely everyone. No one is exempt because everyone from Adam forward is invited to share equally in the renewing and reconciling love of God.

One of the last things Jesus did before he died was forgive a thief dangling on a cross beside him, knowing full well the thief sought help from fear—raw fear. He knew the thief would never study the Bible, attend a church meeting, or make amends to all those he had wronged. He simply said, "Jesus, remember me," (Luke 23:42), and our dying Savior promised, "Today you will be with me in paradise" (Luke 23:43). The mercy of God does not depend on what we do for him but on what he does for us.

Mozart's "Requiem" contains a wonderful line that could be our daily prayer: "Remember, merciful Jesus, that I am the cause of your journey." You can be certain Jesus remembers because he loves us so much.

C. S. Lewis wrote a fictional account of life after death. In *The Great Divorce*, he placed the following words in the mouth of one of his spiritual heroes, George MacDonald:

> Heaven, once attained, will work backwards and turn agony into glory. And that is why at the end of things, the

---

1. Yancey, *What's So Amazing about Grace?*, 62.

Grace

Blessed will say, "We have never lived anywhere except in heaven."[2]

A man was driving down the road and saw a large sign on the front door of a church. He could not read it from the road and was curious enough to drive up to the steps to see what it said. He was surprised to read the following:

Attention! Behind these doors, we worship regularly with liars, thieves, gossips, backbiters, people with troubled marriages, alcoholics, and drug abusers: We welcome hypocritical, jealous, envious, coveting, materialistic sinners of all sizes, shapes, and colors.

There was something else in smaller print that the man could not read from his car, so he got out and walked up closer to read:

But the good news is that we all have something in common. We believe that the church, the body of Christ, is a hospital for sinners, not a museum for saints. You are welcome to join us but be warned that we take our faith seriously.

Because Jesus loves us, we are free to stop pretending. Jesus knows us better than we know ourselves, and he appreciates the ambiguities, the confusion, and the perplexities we face far more than we do.

There is an old rabbinic parable about a farmer who had two sons. As soon as they were old enough to walk, he took them to the fields and taught them everything that he knew about growing crops and raising animals. When he got too old to work, the two boys took over the chores of the farm, and when he died, they had found their work together so meaningful that they decided to keep their partnership. Each brother contributed what he could, and during every harvest season, they would equally divide what they had corporately produced.

Over the years, the elder brother never married. The younger brother did marry and had eight wonderful children. Some years later, when they had a bountiful harvest, the old bachelor brother thought, *my brother has ten mouths to feed. I have only one. He really needs more of the harvest than I do, but I know he is much too*

---

2. Lewis, *The Great Divorce*, 69.

fair to negotiate. I know what I'll do. In the dead of the night, when he is already asleep, I'll take some of what I have put in my barn, and I'll slip it over to his barn to help feed his family.

At the very same time, the younger brother was thinking, *God has given me these wonderful children. My brother has not been so fortunate. He really needs more of this harvest for his old age, but I know him. He is much too fair. He will never negotiate. I know what I will do. In the dead of the night, when he is asleep, I will take some of what I have put in my barn and slip it over to his barn.*

One night, when the moon was full, as you may have already anticipated, those two brothers came face-to-face, each on a mission of generosity. The old rabbi said that there was not a cloud in the sky, but a gentle rain began to fall. You know what it was? God was weeping for joy because two of his children had gotten the point. Two of his children had come to realize that generosity is the deepest characteristic of the holy, and because we are made in God's image, our being generous is the secret to our joy as well. Life is not fair, thank God! It is not fair because it is rooted in grace and mercy and generosity.

A beautiful contemporary parable of God's generosity is the movie *It Could Happen to You*. Imagine a New York City diner. It is time for breakfast, and the diner is crowded with people who are inhaling their food. A New York City policeman is having coffee along with his partner. As he finishes, he reaches into his pocket to pay the bill and leave a tip, but he finds he has only enough to pay for the coffee. There is not enough to leave Yvonne, the waitress, her tip.

Charlie, the cop, is embarrassed and offers Yvonne a choice. He promises to return the next day with double his usual tip—or he will split his lottery ticket winnings should he win "the big one." He did not have money for the tip because he had purchased a lottery ticket earlier that morning.

Yvonne, the waitress, has it bad. She hates her job, her husband left her with so much debt that she had to declare bankruptcy—and now Charlie does not even have enough money for a tip. Yvonne says, "OK, I'll take half of your hoped-for lottery winnings."

Grace

That night, Charlie's lottery ticket wins four million dollars. The next morning, Charlie goes to the diner to give Yvonne the incredible news. Charlie has already had a fight with his wife—and she is outraged that he agreed to give a waitress half of his lottery winnings—but Charlie is an honest guy and intends to keep his word.

You can imagine Yvonne's reaction. As she screams with delight, dancing around the diner to the cheer and applause of her regular customers, she asks Charlie, "Why? You did not have to tell me you won the lottery. You could have kept it all for yourself. Why are you doing this?"

Charlie, the honest cop, answers simply, "Because a promise is a promise."

Yvonne's life is changed forever. She cannot help but be attracted to Charlie—he is honest, generous, and loving—but Charlie is married and faithful to his wife. Of course, Hollywood makes the story turn out well. Charlie's unhappy and bitter wife divorces him mainly because he gave away half of his lottery winnings. In the end, Charlie and Yvonne get together. Yvonne does not just take the money and run like many Christians take God's grace and run. Instead, she does not want just what came through Charlie—she wants Charlie! She wants Charlie for the rest of her life. This honest, generous, loving, promise-keeping man is what she wants most.

In one way, we are all like Yvonne—working in that diner with no way to help ourselves, deeply in debt, and helpless to pay our spiritual debts. Then, in walks Jesus. The love and grace of Jesus walks into our lives and changes us. It also empowers us to live the abundant life. That is especially true for those we deem less worthy of the grace we have received.

I read with interest the commentary surrounding President Trump's choice to lead the prayer at his inauguration on January 20, 2017. Paula White, a twice-divorced Pentecostal "prosperity preacher," has some unorthodox beliefs. She admits that she has made some poor decisions in life and has been less than perfect in her Christian witness. One Christian said, "I would rather hear a Hindu pray than Paula White."

Grace

This all reminds me of something I read in Philip Gulley's *Just Shy of Harmony*. The novel is about a pastor of a small-town Quaker congregation. One of the members of the church is diagnosed with terminal leukemia, and the pastor and the congregation pray earnestly for her healing. However, healing does not come, and she only gets worse.

Some of the church members are avid followers of a greasy televangelist named Johnny LaCosta. He is the kind of guy who pretends to be a vessel of healing if enough seed money is sown into his ministry. So, these church members collect an offering, send it to Johnny LaCosta, and request that he pray for their sick friend.

On television a week or so later, Johnny LaCosta prays for the woman and announces her healed of her leukemia. And, sure enough, the leukemia disappears, and the woman recovers completely. When the Quaker pastor hears that the woman is indeed healed, he becomes angry and refuses to acknowledge that Johnny LaCosta had anything to do with it. God would never work through such a fraud.

A member of the congregation loved her pastor enough to challenge his attitude. "You seem annoyed that she was healed," she said. "What would be wrong with God using Johnny LaCosta to heal Sally?"

Sam, the Quaker minister, sputtered, "First, God didn't use Johnny LaCosta to heal Sally. God doesn't use people like that."

Miriam continued, "I think God can use anyone."

Pastor Sam reluctantly had to confess that maybe God had done something miraculous through such an unworthy vessel as Johnny LaCosta. "I still think he is a bozo," Pastor Sam declared.

"So do I," said Miriam, "but God apparently uses bozos too."[3]

Spiritual arrogance is such an ugly thing. When we think we are usable and others are not, we show that we still do not understand God's amazing grace. One day, hopefully, we will awaken to the fact that God specializes in writing extraordinary stories about very ordinary and sometimes odd, unworthy people like Paula White. And me.

---

3. Gulley, *Just Shy of Harmony*, 238.

Grace

It might be a good thing to go easy on all your bozos. God just might do something through them to remind you that without Christ, you too do not have a prayer. The introduction to a children's Bible I purchased for my grandchildren sums things up nicely:

> People think the Bible is a book of heroes, showing you people you should copy. The Bible does have some heroes in it, but . . . most of the people in the Bible aren't heroes at all. They make some big mistakes (sometimes on purpose). They get afraid and run away. At times, they are downright mean. No, the Bible isn't a book of rules, or a book of heroes. The Bible is most of all a Story. It's an adventure story about a young Hero who comes from a far country to win back his lost treasure. It's a love story about a brave Prince who leaves his palace, his throne—everything—to rescue the one he loves.[4]

God is the hero of every story—even yours and mine.

---

4. Lloyd-Jones, *The Jesus Storybook Bible*, 14–16.

12

Metanarrative

And there were shepherds living out in the fields nearby, keeping watch over their flocks at night. An angel of the Lord appeared to them, and the glory of the Lord shone around them, and they were terrified. But the angel said to them, "Do not be afraid. I bring you good news of great joy that will be for all the people. Today in the town of David a Savior has been born to you; he is the Messiah, the Lord. This will be a sign to you: You will find a baby wrapped in cloths and lying in a manger." Suddenly a great company of the heavenly host appeared with the angel, praising God and saying, "Glory to God in the highest heaven, and on earth peace to those on whom his favor rests."

—LUKE 2:8–14

The story of Creation, Fall, Redemption, and New Creation is one we need to read often. It's the story of God's faithfulness and goodness. And because we know the Author of the story personally and trust his will, we can watch the story of

Metanarrative

our lives unfold with wonder and awe. Even when we get to a scene that is confusing or seems out of place, we can remember, wait, watch, knowing that the story is moving forward to a beautiful and glorious end. Jesus made it so when he signed the manuscript with his own blood and said, "It is finished!"

—CHRISTINA FOX

WHITE CHRISTMAS IS THE most popular Christmas song ever recorded. In fact, until 1997, it was the best-selling song of all time. Elton John's remake of *A Candle in the Wind*, a tribute to Princess Diana, would eventually outsell *White Christmas*.

Irving Berlin's *White Christmas* was first heard on a radio show on Christmas Day in 1941. Families tuning in to that broadcast were no doubt thinking about the tragic event that happened just eighteen days earlier—the attack on Pearl Harbor. By the following winter, young American troops were overseas, and Armed Forces Radio played *White Christmas* over and over to remind them of home and the cause for which they were fighting.

Most do not know that the composer of *White Christmas*, Irving Berlin, did not himself celebrate Christmas. He was Jewish and had emigrated to the United Stated from Russia as a child. Christmas was a sad day for Irving Berlin. While Christians all over America were celebrating and opening gifts, Irving Berlin had his own tradition. Every year, he visited the grave of his son who died on Christmas Day in 1928. Perhaps Christmas Day, in some way, gave this grieving Jewish father some type of hope or peace.

There is always a backstory to any story. In Luke's account of the birth of Jesus, Rome dominated the world. We have many Roman records from that period, including official records and dispatches from the far-flung provinces reporting what happened in the Roman Empire. However, nowhere is it mentioned that a baby named Jesus was born to a peasant couple named Joseph and Mary in a little town called Bethlehem in a province called Judea.

Metanarrative

You cannot find any record of it anywhere in any official document—not a word.

But here it is in the second chapter of Luke's Gospel because Luke is writing the backstory, the behind-the-scenes history of the first century. Luke has tapped into the bigger story, the metanarrative, the story behind earth's little story. Luke, like any historian, has a particular bias in telling his version of the Christmas story.

Luke sees history from the perspective of the poor, the marginalized, and the forgotten. It behooves us to remember that when God took on human flesh, he took on poor flesh. Things are not always as they seem. Luke wants us to realize that. He begins where you must begin if you are writing a history of the first century. He begins with Rome, the most dominating power in the history of the world at that time. You have got to begin with Rome:

> In those days Caesar Augustus issued a decree that a census should be taken of the entire Roman world. (This was the first census that took place while Quirinius was governor of Syria). And everyone went to their own town to register. So, Joseph went up from the town of Nazareth in Galilee to Judea, to Bethlehem, the town of David, because he belonged to the house and line of David. He went there to register with Mary, who was pledged to be married to him and was expecting a child. While they were there, the time came for the baby to be born, and she gave birth to her firstborn, a son (Luke 2:1–7).

Luke begins reporting what seems to be on center stage, but he moves immediately to another story, a backstory, a story behind Rome's story, the bigger story, God's story. From that story, he reports that there was another announcement given at the same time, in the same year, but it was not an announcement from Caesar. This announcement is from heaven, and it is not addressed to the whole Roman world but to a group of shepherds on a hillside not far from Bethlehem. Here is the irony. When Rome spoke, it addressed the entire empire, but when heaven spoke, it addressed only a select few.

Metanarrative

Jews hated the Roman census. In fact, any census was met with resistance by the Jews. Why? Because the Jews still bitterly remembered the census King David had tried to enforce centuries earlier:

> Satan rose up against Israel and incited David to take a census of Israel (1 Chronicles 21:1).

This occurred immediately following a great victory over the Philistines, and the text implies that David was displaying pride and self-reliance. The census would allow David to draft soldiers and levy taxes. He was moving away from humble reliance on God, and for this, God disciplined both David and the nation of Israel. Any mention of a census angered Jews, and this Roman census would galvanize a resistance into a political movement called the Zealot Party, which would eventually wage guerrilla warfare against Rome, leading to Rome's destruction of Jerusalem in AD 70.

The Roman census was bad news, but in the midst of such bad news, an angel appeared to a lowly group of shepherds:

> I bring you good news of great joy that will be for all the people. (Luke 2:10).

Luke wants us to ponder these competing narratives: the lesser story in the decree of Caesar Augustus delivering the same old bad news and the larger narrative in the angelic proclamation announcing good tidings of great joy.

It is clear God is in control of history. Caesar's decree brought Mary and Joseph to Bethlehem, thus fulfilling Micah's prophecy:

> But you, Bethlehem Ephrathah, though you are small among the clans of Judah, out of you will come for me one who will be ruler over Israel, whose origins are from old, from ancient times (Micah 5:2).

God's bigger story, the metanarrative, is God in control, directing the drama of the ages.

Do you believe, as I believe, that God is at work in our world, in our lives, as he was in the lives of Mary and Joseph, the shepherds, and Caesar Augustus? Do you believe there is indeed

Metanarrative

a bigger story, a metanarrative, behind the scenes amid both our good and bad days?

Not long ago, I conducted the funeral of a beautiful thirty-eight-year-old nurse who died after a long and courageous battle with cancer. She loved nature and God's animal kingdom, and she was fully dedicated to being a partner in the healing ministry of Jesus. What do you say when loving parents ask the age-old question: Why?

I told my good friends that I did not know why God would allow their precious daughter to die any more than I know why he allowed our daughter to die. I then told them the two things that have kept my family moving forward after having faced similar heartache. We believe without question that:

1. God is good.
2. God's overall plan is good (regardless of our children's deaths).

Romans 8:28 (In all things God is working for good) is our lifeline, promising that in the midst of all the good and evil that we will experience in life, and in the lives of the ones we love, God is at work for good.

My Utmost for His Highest is one of the most popular devotionals ever published. Its author, Oswald Chambers, died while serving in Egypt at the age of forty-three, following surgery for a ruptured appendix. His death was a great shock to those closest to him. Why would God take Oswald Chambers at such an early age when there were so few men like him?

> On the day of his funeral, his wife Biddy remembered a conversation they had while he was polishing his boots the week before. They had just returned from the hospital where they had visited a friend, a woman named Gertrude Ballinger suffering from typhoid fever and near death. Biddy said to Oswald, "I wonder what God is going to do with Gertrude." Oswald, between brushstrokes, said to his wife, "I don't care what God does. It's what God is that I care about."[1]

---

1. McCasland, *Oswald Chambers: Abandoned to God*, 13.

Metanarrative

No doubt, those words had lodged in Biddy's mind to help her accept and bear her husband's unexpected death just a week after their hospital visit. Knowing that God is good is better than understanding what God does.

Through the years, God has given our family "gentle whispers" that keep pulling us forward, confirming what we have always believed: that nothing will hinder God's good story. Nothing, not even death.

Shortly after our daughter's death in 1993, we decided to remain in the United States and not return to Brazil. Returning to pastoral ministry in North Carolina, we decided to buy a home. The very first house we were scheduled to see seemed perfect. It was in a good neighborhood. There was a lake and a playground nearby. The house had four bedrooms. The fourth bedroom would have been for Alexandra, but it would now be used for our many guests.

We knew that this was meant to be our house when we entered it for the first time. Going upstairs, we began to examine the bedrooms. One of them stood out because it was painted the ugliest shade of aqua that you can imagine, which just happened to be Alex's favorite color. We never understood why she loved aqua so much. Now we do. God was reminding us that she is with us because God is with us:

> God is not the God of the dead but of the living (Matthew 22:32).

Another "gentle whisper" was that for several weeks before Alex died, she kept reminding us of things we had forgotten and things we had enjoyed together in Brazil. She was steadfast in asking, "Do you remember?" It was as though she was refreshing our memories to give us strength for the journey. I can assure you that I am not in denial. I am not stuck in one of the many stages of grief. I grieve as deeply as anyone who has buried a child. I simply long for more than this world has to offer. Longing to see how God is going to bring his good story to an end helps me endure. It keeps me going with great hope and expectation.[2]

2. Hipps, *When A Child Dies*, 35–36.

Metanarrative

It is not natural to treasure the invisible over the visible or the eternal promises of God over the temporal promises of this world. It takes born-again eyes to see the difference. Demas, Paul's companion, deserted him and the work of spreading the gospel. Why?

> Demas, because he loved this world, has deserted me and has gone to Thessalonica (2 Timothy 4:10).

I believe part of the reason for this is that God's promises seem so distant. Unlike our Lord Jesus, we have none of his memories of heaven. However, we still have the witness of the apostle Paul who encourages us to take the long view:

> Therefore we do not lose heart. Though outwardly we are wasting away, yet inwardly we are being renewed day by day. For our light and momentary troubles are achieving for us an eternal glory that far outweighs them all. So we fix our eyes not on what is seen, but what is unseen, since what is seen is temporary, but what is unseen is eternal (2 Corinthians 4:16–18).

Joni Eareckson Tada is the spiritual hero of so many, especially those with disabilities, those who have had it harder than most. In *Heaven: Your Real Home . . . From a Higher Perspective*, she speaks for most of these individuals whose lives compel them to keep looking forward:

> After a week of wheelchair hikes, Bible studies, and arts and crafts, I listened as the microphone was passed from family to family, each tearfully sharing how wonderful the time had been. Some talked of meeting new friends. Others, of the games, music, and hikes. A few confessed that they wished the week would just go on and on.
>
> Then little red-haired, freckled-faced Jeff raised his hand. He had Down Syndrome and had won the hearts of many adults at the retreat. People had been captivated by his winsome smile and joyful spirit. Everyone leaned forward to hear his words. Jeff grabbed the mike and kept it short and sweet as he bellowed, 'Let's go home!' He smiled, bowed, and handed back the microphone. All the families roared with laughter.

Metanarrative

His mother told me later that, even though Jeff thoroughly immersed himself in the week's festivities, he missed his daddy back home.

I identify with Jeff. The good things in this world are pleasant enough, but would we really wish for it to go on as it is? I don't think so. The nice things in this life are merely omens, foreshadowings, of even greater, more glorious things to come.[3]

I am with Jeff and Joni and the apostle Paul:

> If only for this life we have hope in Christ, we are to be pitied more than all others (1 Corinthians 15:19).

---

3. Eareckson Tada, *Heaven: Your Real Home*, 181–82.

13

Galilee

When the Sabbath was over, Mary Magdalene, Mary the mother of James, and Salome bought spices so that they might go to anoint Jesus's body. Very early on the first day of the week, just after sunrise, they were on their way to the tomb and they asked each other, "Who will roll the stone away from the entrance of the tomb?" But when they looked up, they saw that the stone, which was very large, had been rolled away. As they entered the tomb, they saw a young man dressed in a white robe sitting on the right side, and they were alarmed. "Don't be alarmed," he said. "You are looking for Jesus the Nazarene, who was crucified. He has risen! He is not here. See the place where they laid him. But go, tell his disciples and Peter, 'He is going ahead of you into Galilee. There you will see him, just as he told you.'" Trembling and bewildered, the women went out and fled from the tomb. They said nothing to anyone, because they were afraid.

—Mark 16:1–8

Galilee

Jesus prevents us from thinking that life is a matter of ideas to ponder or concepts to discuss. Jesus saves us from wasting our lives in the pursuit of cheap thrills and trivializing diversions. Jesus enables us to take seriously who we are and where we are without being seduced by the intimidating lies and illusions that fill the air, so that we needn't be someone else or somewhere else. Jesus keeps our feet on the ground, attentive to children, in conversation with ordinary people, sharing meals with friends and strangers, listening to the wind, observing the wildflowers, touching the sick and wounded, praying simply and unselfconsciously. Jesus insists that we deal with God right here and now, in the place we find ourselves and with the people we are with. Jesus is God here and now.

—EUGENE H. PETERSON

HAVE YOU EVER GONE to a movie and sat through the entire film when all of a sudden, the movie abruptly ends? You think, *What? That's it? Did I miss something? What kind of ending is that? I sat here for two hours—and that is it?*

I vividly remember sitting in the theater when *The Empire Strikes Back* was ending. Darth Vader had just told Luke, "I am your father." I thought, *What? No, do not end the movie now. I cannot wait for three years to find out what this means!*

That kind of ending reminds me of *The Lady or the Tiger* by Frank R. Stockton, which most of us read in high school. Originally published in 1882 in *The Century*, we read of a princess who falls in love with a lowly commoner, and her father is furious and has the man arrested.

Justice would be dispensed by placing the accused man in a stadium facing two doors. Behind one door was a hungry tiger waiting to pounce, and behind the other door was a beautiful woman. The accused would have to choose one of the doors to determine guilt or innocence.

If he chose the door with the tiger, he would be mauled to death and ruled guilty. If he chose the door with the beautiful woman, he would be wed to her on the spot—no matter his current relational status. In the story, the princess discovered what was behind each door, but she was torn. She could not bear the thought of losing the only man she had ever loved to another woman, but the thought of him being ripped apart by a hungry tiger was equally painful.

As the accused man stood in the stadium facing the two doors, he glanced up at the princess. She gestured to the right, and the story ended there. Did she send him to his death—or did she forfeit the love of her life to another woman? Of course, the writer left the ending unresolved to encourage the reader to contemplate the two possibilities. Was the princess moved by her compassion or her jealousy?

In high school, I hated this story. I did not like having to speculate, and the class discussion afterward made things even more complicated and frustrating. I wanted the writer to be specific and clear and give me a good answer that made perfect sense. He did not.

Apparently, some later editors of Mark's Gospel felt like me when they read Mark's ending. In our oldest manuscripts, Mark's Gospel ends with chapter 16, verse 8:

> Trembling and bewildered, the women went out and fled from the tomb. They said nothing to anyone, because they were afraid.

This is not exactly the ending most of us look for. At least in the Gospels of Matthew, Luke, and John, Jesus shows up again.

The ending of any story is crucial. We want the team to win, the hero to live, the relationship to blossom, and the crime to be solved. Those endings that blindside us can be disappointing, but I have been thinking. Those stories with neat, tidy endings might satisfy at the time, but they rarely transform us or cause us to stop

Galilee

and reflect. Only stories with unclear endings invite us into finishing the story for ourselves.

And that is what we have in the Gospel of Mark—a promise of Jesus's resurrection that ends in fear and awe—and maybe that is the point of Mark's abrupt and displeasing ending. He knows the truth about us—that our lives are so often lived in moments just like that—moments of fear and awe. And we have to admire Mark's genius, under the inspiration of the Holy Spirit, to step aside at the last minute, hand us the pen, and say, "Here, you write it, write a resurrection conclusion with your own life." Brilliant!

We seem to be living in a culture and time when all we want are quick and easy answers. Here is a list of things you need to know. Here are the facts you need to memorize. Here are the things you need to get into your head. Scripture is not interested in that formula; it does not always lead us to answers. Instead, it invites us to enter the story.

This is hard for some of us because in many ways, we want our faith to be an easy list of things to believe. We believe this about God and that about the Bible, and this is good. But if you really pay attention to what happened in those early years of the church, you'll see that the followers of Jesus were more interested in inviting people into the story than they were about giving people a boatload of answers. Answers can be idols.

So, here we are in the twenty-first century, trying to make sense of Mark's abrupt ending, and in doing so, we have to dig a little deeper. Mark does give us a few clues that his story (the oldest of the Gospels) is intended to be a story without an ending. He does not want us to be satisfied. He does not want us to have closure. We are being invited to go deeper—to enter the story ourselves.

Mark's version of Easter is almost like a crime scene. Think about it. We have an open grave and a missing body. We have a witness at the scene, but we do not know how credible. We have this young man dressed in white sitting inside the tomb, inside the yellow tape, crime scene already contaminated. But this witness has some inside information—information that would be hard for anyone outside of Jesus's inner circle to know. He knows the

Galilee

disciples by their names. He knows why the women are there. And then he gives the women his most important clue. The witness says that the key to understanding Easter is *Galilee*.

> He is going ahead of you into Galilee. There you will see him, just as he told you (Mark 16:7).

Jesus had told his disciples something about Galilee while he was still with them. It was when they were on the Mount of Olives right after the Last Supper, right before Jesus was arrested:

> But, after I have risen, I will go ahead of you into Galilee (Mark 14:28).

What was so special about Galilee? It was home to both Jesus and his disciples. Jesus, "the man from Galilee," grew up in the village of Nazareth. By choosing Galilee, Jesus was bringing the resurrection home, back to where the story began.

In the opening chapter of Mark's Gospel, verse 14, Jesus went into Galilee to proclaim the good news of God. Mark is deliberately taking us back to the beginning—this time as participants in the narrative. The disciples' betrayal, denial, desertion, and lack of trust are not the end of the story. Galilee equals a fresh start, a do-over, the opportunity to begin again. All life experiences can now be understood afresh in light of the resurrection.

Interestingly, Jesus does not say he will accompany the disciples back to Galilee; he will go ahead of them. He is always ahead of us. Before we breathe a prayer, shed a tear, or seek forgiveness, he is ahead of us. Galilee is a metaphor for those past, personal, and intimate places in our lives where we met our Lord and were forever changed. We all have our own *Galilees* and they grow in number as the years go by. Mentally returning to those special places builds our trust and confirms God's call on our life, reaffirming his faithfulness from the beginning.

In C. S. Lewis's *The Chronicles of Narnia*, four children travel from England through a wardrobe to the new world of Narnia and meet Aslan, a great lion. Aslan is a symbol for Christ, and in the first book, with Aslan's help, the children defeat the white witch who held the land of Narnia in perpetual winter. In the second book, they help Prince Caspian return to his rightful throne. By the third book, the children have grown to love both Narnia and Aslan deeply, but Aslan tells them it is their last trip to Narnia—and they can never return. Lucy, the youngest of the children, is heartbroken at the idea of not seeing Aslan again. But Aslan tells Lucy that she will see him again back in England in her ordinary life. Wherever she goes, Aslan will meet her there.

He will also meet you wherever you are. Maybe as you are having an MRI, in the waiting room when someone you love is in surgery, in a chair taking chemotherapy, in a lawyer's office discussing divorce, or, in a counselor's office because you think you are being crushed by life. Jesus has gone ahead of you and will meet you there—in the thick of life.

Mark, the first and oldest Gospel, gives us the resurrection story with an open ending, an ending that requires us to fill in the blanks. We are faced with a dilemma like what we experienced in high school when we read "The Lady or the Tiger" for the first time. Did the princess succumb to jealousy and point her lover to the tiger—or did she give him up to another woman to save his life? As teenagers, we learned that the point of the story was not about the choice the princess had to make; it is about the choice we make.

As much as you and I dislike ambiguity, isn't that what we face so often in life? Life is full of uncertainty, full of choices that are difficult to make, but the promise we have is that the risen Christ goes before us wherever life takes us. Mark's gospel closes with a choice but not an ending. It is not about what the women at the tomb will do, it is about what *we* will do. Each of us has been given the same message by the angel at the tomb:

- He has been raised.
- He is not here.
- He is going ahead of you.

14

Trust

That day when evening came, he said to his disciples, "Let us go over to the other side." Leaving the crowd behind, they took him along, just as he was, in the boat. There were also other boats with him. A furious squall came up, and the waves broke over the boat, so that it was nearly swamped. Jesus was in the stern, sleeping on a cushion. The disciples woke him and said to him, "Teacher, don't you care if we drown?" He got up, rebuked the wind and said to the waves, "Quiet! Be still!" Then the wind died down and it was completely calm. He said to his disciples, "Why are you so afraid? Do you still have no faith?" They were terrified and asked each other, "Who is this? Even the wind and the waves obey him!"

—Mark 4:35–41

"Yea, though I walk through the valley of the shadow of death, I will fear no evil." The psalm does not pretend that evil and death do not exist. Terrible things happen, and they happen to good people. Even the paths of righteousness lead through the valley of the shadow. Death lies ahead of all of us, saints and sinners alike, and for all the ones we love. The psalmist doesn't try to explain evil. He simply says he will not fear evil. For all the power that evil has, it doesn't have the power to make him afraid. And why? Here at the very center of the psalmist's faith, suddenly he stops speaking about God as "he," because you don't speak that way when the person is right there with you. Suddenly he speaks to God instead of about him, and he speaks to him as "Thou." "I will fear no evil," he says, "for Thou art with me." That is the center of faith. Thou. That is where faith comes from.

—Frederick Buechner

The most repeated command in scripture is not the command to love, the command to pray, the command to give, or even the command to seek the lost. The most repeated command in scripture is fear not!

Do you own a Kindle? Amazon tracks this, and the most underlined passage in every version of the Bible is Philippians 4:6–7:

> Do not be anxious about anything, but in every situation, by prayer and petition, with thanksgiving, present your requests to God. And the peace of God, which transcends all understanding, will guard your hearts and your minds in Christ Jesus.

I have always believed that there are two primary emotions: love and fear. We choose to walk in one or the other daily.

Knowing all of this, there was a time in my life when I was completely overcome with fear and anxiety. While Patricia and I were in language school in Campinas, Brazil, we got word that a very special friend and fellow missionary had been killed in a plane crash in Cuenca, Ecuador. Here is the *Baptist Press* release from July 11, 1983:

> Southern Baptist missionary Roger L. Thompson, 35, was among 116 persons presumed killed July 1 in the crash of a Boeing 737 airliner just two minutes before its scheduled arrival in Cuenca.
>
> Thompson, of Linthicum Heights, MD, was en route to direct a meeting at First Baptist Church, Cuenca, in the use of a soul-winners' New Testament in evangelistic witnessing.
>
> Thompson's wife, the former Susan C. Rich, and their three children were in the United States visiting her parents. The Thompsons' home in Quito had been badly damaged in a five-foot-deep mudslide April 30 and they had been living in temporary quarters.
>
> Mrs. Thompson and the children had planned to return to Ecuador July 14. In addition to Mrs. Thompson and the children; Rachel, 8, Derek, 6, and Rebecca, almost 3, survivors include his parents, Mr. and Mrs. Sylvester Thompson of Linthicum Heights.

Roger Thompson was not just a friend; he was an important mentor in missions while I was a student at Southeastern Baptist Theological Seminary in Wake Forest, North Carolina. I followed Roger as fellow to Dr. James Leo Green, distinguished professor of Old Testament Studies, who also encouraged Patricia and me to consider missions in Brazil. Dr. Green had spent several weeks teaching in the Baptist Theological Seminary in Rio de Janeiro, and I knew they needed a professor of Christian ethics. I was appointed to fill that position the following year.

Roger Thompson helped me make that decision, and now, he was dead? Killed in a plane crash on his way to teach people how to share their faith? How could this be? I have never known anyone more passionate about his call, yet, for some reason, God permitted him to die tragically—along with 115 other helpless passengers. It shook me to the core. It was a major crisis of faith for me. I figured if this man, this on-fire totally dedicated missionary, could die in a plane crash, then so could I.

A spirit of fear came over me, and I became petrified at the thought of flying. Being afraid to fly is a handicap for a missionary. When I knew I would have to fly anywhere, I would obsess and worry about it for weeks. It did a number on me. I became anxious about being anxious. I lost sleep, lost my appetite, and sadly, lost my joy.

It all came to a head when I had to fly to Rio de Janeiro for a meeting. At the time we lived in the southernmost state of Brazil (Rio Grande do Sul) in the capital city of Porto Alegre. It is a two-hour flight from there to Rio, and I was a nervous wreck for weeks. When I boarded the flight, I was more anxious than I had ever been. I prayed not to have a major panic attack during the flight. I barely made it to Rio, and I was not sure if I could get back on the plane for the return trip two weeks later. Those were two of the most miserable weeks I have ever spent obsessing and worrying. I worried about being worried, and I feared being afraid, which totally distracted me from enjoying one of the most beautiful cities in the world.

When the day came to return home, I was too embarrassed to admit what I was suffering internally as one of my good friends dropped me off at the airport. I had to board the plane, and I prayed for the strength to do so. As I sat down in my window seat, I thought, *if we are going to crash, I want to see it coming.* A gentleman sat down in the aisle seat of my row, and no one occupied the middle seat.

I closed my eyes and prayed: *Lord, I am so scared. I am worried about my family, and I do not want to leave them alone. Lord, help me be free of this fear and feel your peace.*

We took off—without crashing—leveled off, and the flight attendant came to take our drink orders. The man in the aisle seat requested a Coke in English, and I asked, "Sir, are you from the States?"

"Yes, are you an American?" he asked.

"Yes," I said. "I'm a Baptist missionary living in Porto Alegre."

I will never forget what happened next. The man reached over the empty seat and grabbed my arm. "This is an answer to prayer," he said. "I am in the shoe industry, and this is my first time overseas. I am so afraid of flying, but of course, I could not tell my employer. Isn't that awful, Pastor?"

Trust

I said, "You are afraid of flying? Why? It is the safest travel on earth!"

What he said then changed my life.

"Pastor, I am ashamed to admit my fear, and I prayed God would let me sit next to a person of faith to give me courage. And God sent you. I have not slept since I left Miami. I am so exhausted, and I am going to sleep these last two hours in peace. Please tell the flight attendant not to wake me when they serve lunch." He slept like a baby all the way to Porto Alegre.

As Jesus calmed the storm on the Sea of Galilee that day, he calmed the storm within me. "Peace be still," he said, and my anxiety subsided. From that day forward, I decided I would never allow anxiety to have the upper hand whether I died in a plane crash or not. God's playfulness in sending me to help this anxious businessman from Boston was his reminder that his perfect love is all that I will ever need to face my fears. The apostle John is right, perfect love drives out fear (1 John 4:18). I will never forget the personal, humorous, loving way God drove out my fear at ten thousand feet.

In John Bunyan's *Pilgrim's Progress,* there is a character named Mr. Fearing. It was said that he "lived his journey without joy and missed out on all the better songs." Does that sound like you? I hope not. Jesus came to save us and to give us an abundant life that is overflowing with joy and peace and the stability of Christ himself.

Our Lord wants us to live to the fullest, and that cannot happen if we are paralyzed with fear and anxiety. Fear and anxiety stifle our capacity to think clearly and rationally, lead to indecision that amplifies our angst, diminish our ability to perform well in various situations, cause us to forget that God's plan is unfolding—fulfilling his sovereign purposes—and can become the basis for numerous health problems.

So, how are we going to live without being paralyzed by fear and anxiety? The same way Jesus did. How did he do it?

- He had an eternal perspective.
- He had unconditional trust in God's sovereign plan.
- He accepted that life on earth would never be safe.

Trust

Let us examine these one by one. First, Jesus had an eternal perspective:

> Look at the birds of the air; they do not sow or reap or store away in barns, and yet your heavenly Father feeds them. Are you not much more valuable than they? (Matthew 6:26).

According to our Lord, we humans are much more important than little birds because we are made in God's image:

> Are not two sparrows sold for a penny? Yet not one of them will fall to the ground outside your Father's care. And even the very hairs of your head are all numbered. So don't be afraid; you are worth more than many sparrows (Matthew 10:29–31).

The primary focus of little birds is this world, the only world they know. We, on the other hand, are the children of light made not just for this world but also for another world. What are the metaphors that best describe us? Pilgrim, sojourner, tent-dweller, and traveler. Our Lord Jesus confirmed this in his high priestly prayer in John 17:15–16:

> My prayer is not that you take them out of the world but that you protect them from the evil one. They are not of the world, even as I am not of it.

The apostle Paul admonishes us to:

> So we fix our eyes not on what is seen, but what is unseen, since what is seen is temporary, but what is unseen is eternal (2 Corinthians 4:18).

Jesus believed in a bigger story than dying in a storm on a lake along with his frightened disciples. He would die, and he knew it, but not on that lake. That is why he slept soundly, and after being awakened, he lovingly reprimanded his disciples for their shortsighted, earthbound thinking.

> He said to his disciples, "Why are you so afraid? Do you still have no faith?" (Mark 4:40).

Trust

I have been preaching for years that our good God is telling a good story that will have a good ending. I will go to my grave believing this. Jesus's whole life was a life lived with childlike trust in his Father's goodness. You cannot have an intimate walk with God unless you believe God is good.

How many of us who call ourselves followers of Jesus really believe that God is good all the time? If we are honest there are times when we are tempted to doubt the goodness of God.

- If God is good, why did he . . . ?
- If God is good, why hasn't he . . . ?
- If God is good, why won't he . . . ?

These types of questions illustrate what the apostle Paul calls the carnal mind. We imagine the best life possible, based on worldly comforts and benefits, and then we imagine it's God's job to give us those good things.

The carnal mind is the one that hears "God is good" and secretly thinks, *let me sift through the evidence of my experience, and then I'll decide if that's true.* What we need instead is the humble attitude that says to God, "I am in no condition or position to judge you or your character." If we are following the example of our Lord, we will say, "No matter what happens, I will stand on the truth that God is good—and I will wait for God's goodness to play itself out even if I have to wait until I get to heaven."

Think about it. What helped Jesus accept and embrace the cross? Was it not his unwavering belief in God's goodness?

> And let us run with perseverance the race marked out for us, fixing our eyes on Jesus, the pioneer and perfecter of faith. For the joy set before him he endured the cross, scorning its shame, and sat down at the right hand of the throne of God (Hebrews 12:1–2).

The joy of knowing that God's good plan was unfolding enabled Jesus to bear what he did. The same kind of trust will also provide what we need to bear what we must as we go through life.

Trust

The beautiful hymn, "O Love That Will Not Let Me Go," invites us to believe that all ends well:

> O Joy that seekest me through pain,
> I cannot close my heart to thee;
> I trace the rainbow through the rain,
> and feel the promise is not vain
> that morn shall tearless be.

Are you tempted to doubt God's goodness because of some unanswered prayer? Some great loss? Some great pain? Do not fall into that trap. Be like Jesus. He refused to doubt and chose a childlike confidence in the goodness of God. It is he who taught us that our God is a good God who is telling a good story with a good ending.

I love what C. S. Lewis said in *God in the Dock*:

> In *Hamlet*, a branch breaks and Ophelia is drowned. Did she die because the branch broke or because Shakespeare, the author, wanted her to die at that point in the play?[1]

We come close to believing God has failed in some way when someone dies, but scripture says, "Precious in the sight of the Lord is the death of those faithful to him" (Psalm 116:15).

Why is it so hard for us to believe that? Psalm 116:15 does not say, "Precious in the sight of the Lord is the death of those faithful to him, who live pain-free lives and die in their sleep at the age of one hundred." It says, "those faithful to him," and that includes our little four-year-old Alexandra who went home to heaven in 1993. Was her death "good" in the temporal sense? No, of course not. We have missed her madly these many, many years.

However, because we believe that our God is a good God telling a good story, we will wait in faith for the good ending. The worst thing that happens to us will not be the last thing. God will write the final paragraph, and I can hardly wait to see how things end.

A second reason Jesus was never paralyzed with fear and anxiety is because he had unconditional trust in God's sovereign

---

1. Lewis, *God in the Dock*, 79.

Trust

plan. This is a great challenge for us: unwavering, unconditional trust in God's sovereignty.

A writer I enjoy, Barbara Brown Taylor, tells the story about when she was on a barrier island where loggerhead turtles were laying their eggs. One night, when the tide was out, she watched a huge female turtle heave herself up the beach to dig her nest and empty herself into it. Not wanting to disturb her, Taylor went back to her hotel.

The next morning, she returned to the same spot and noticed that the turtle, instead of returning to the sea, had become disoriented and had wandered into the dunes, which were already hot as asphalt in the morning sun. A little way inland, Taylor found her exhausted and all but baked. Her head and flippers were caked with dry sand. After pouring water on her, she left and found a park ranger who returned to rescue her.

As Taylor watched, the ranger flipped the turtle over on her back, wrapped tire chains around her legs, and hooked the chains to his trailer hitch on his jeep. Then he took off, yanking her body forward toward the ocean. The poor turtle's mouth was filled with sand and her head was so bent that Taylor feared her neck would break.

When the ranger got the turtle down onto the beach, he unhooked her and turned her over again. She lay motionless in the surf as the water lapped at her body, washing the sand from her eyes and mouth. Then a particularly large wave broke over her, and she lifted her head slightly. With every fresh wave, she seemed to revive. Watching her swim away and remembering her nightmare ride through the dunes, Taylor noted that it is sometimes hard to tell whether you are being killed or being saved by the hands that turned your life upside down.[2]

Friend, if you are presently being dragged through the dunes, never doubt that you are in good hands. Like Jesus, have an unwavering, unconditional trust in God's sovereign plan. Remind yourself daily that you have been written into a good story by a

---

2. Brown Taylor, *Learning to Walk in the Dark*, 66–67.

good God who guarantees a good ending. Our final destination is well worth the rough ride.

And finally, like Jesus, we must accept that life on earth will never be safe. Sparrows fall to the ground, as do airplanes, and some caskets will be small caskets. There are no guarantees in this life for any of us. Our security is in Jesus and not in our safety. Security, biblical security, is not about safety. Bad things are going to happen to us all:

> I have told you these things, so that in me you may have peace. In this world you will have trouble. But take heart! I have overcome the world (John 16:33).

We are not safe in this world, but we are loved—and that love is powerful enough to cast out fear of any bad thing having the last word.

I encourage you to meditate deeply on the words of Romans 8:35–39. These verses remind us of just how secure—not safe—we are in the love of God:

> Who shall separate us from the love of Christ? Shall trouble or hardship or persecution or famine or nakedness or danger or sword? As it is written: "For your sake we face death all day long; we are considered as sheep to be slaughtered." No, in all these things we are more than conquerors through him who loved us. For I am convinced that neither death nor life, neither angels or demons, neither the present nor the future, nor any powers, neither height nor depth, nor anything else in all creation will be able to separate us from the love of God that is in Christ Jesus our Lord.

The old hymn says, "safe and secure from all alarms." Notice how the writer says we are safe from alarms—not harm. That is good theology and very biblical. Security is not about safety. It is about trust. Trust that no matter what this unsafe world throws at us, we are eternally secure in the love of Jesus.

These are the words carved on the tombstone of our youngest child, Leigh Alexandra. They are taken from her favorite story, *The Lion, the Witch, and the Wardrobe* by C. S. Lewis:

Trust

> Wrong will be right when Aslan comes in sight,
> At the sound of his roar, sorrows will be no more,
> When he bares his teeth, winter meets its death,
> And when he shakes his mane, we will have spring again.

Spring is coming! The eternal love of Jesus guarantees it. Safe and secure from all alarms.

15

Angels

This is how the birth of Jesus the Messiah came about: His mother Mary was pledged to be married to Joseph, but before they came together, she was found to be pregnant through the Holy Spirit. Because Joseph her husband was a righteous man and did not want to expose her to public disgrace, he had in mind to divorce her quietly. But after he had considered this, an angel of the Lord appeared to him in a dream and said, "Joseph, son of David, do not be afraid to take Mary home as your wife, because what is conceived in her is from the Holy Spirit. She will give birth to a son, and you are to give him the name Jesus, because he will save his people from their sins."

—Matthew 1:18–21

Do not forget to show hospitality to strangers, for by so doing some people have shown hospitality to angels without knowing it.

—Hebrews 13:2

Angels

> Slight-of-hand-magic is based on the demonstrable fact that as a rule people see only what they expect to see. Angels are powerful spirits whom God sends into the world to wish us well. Since we don't expect to see them, we don't. An angel spreads its glittering wings over us, and we say things like, "It was one of those days that made you feel good just to be alive," or "I had a hunch everything was going to turn out alright," or "I don't know where I ever found the courage."
>
> —Frederick Buechner

Do you believe in angels? Do you believe angels are present right here, right now, perhaps reading these words with you? Are they as active in our world today as they were in biblical times? When we get to heaven, will we meet the angels that have helped us and discover the many times they were guiding, guarding, and inspiring us? What stories will they tell us about our best and worst days? What difference will it make in our day-to-day lives if we truly believe angels are not just real but helping keep us faithful and moving forward?

My godly grandmother told me a story I will never forget. When she was about ten years old, she had prepared some food for her father while he was working in a rock quarry. Her mother had died four years earlier, and my grandmother assisted in the preparation of meals and helped raise her younger brother.

To get to the quarry, she had to cross a long bridge over a river. Granny was terrified of the bridge, and on that day, she was so overcome with fear that she sat down and began to cry. Unexpectedly, a voice said, "Honey, if you're afraid to cross the bridge, I'll walk with you." Standing by her was a man holding the reins of a horse. He looked quite normal, but in Granny's words, "His eyes were so bright and so comforting." No longer afraid, she walked across the bridge with the kind stranger and his horse. Their conversation was casual, discussing especially the blue sky. As they approached the

Angels

end of the bridge, Granny turned to thank the man for his company. And before her eyes, both man and horse vanished!

My grandmother lived into her mid-eighties and recalled this special day in her life as one of the gifts given to her by a gracious God to prepare her for the hard days she would face. All her life, she knew there was more.

In the modern church, stories such as these are seldom heard. There seems to be an aversion to the supernatural. We have downgraded our vision of heaven and lost interest in God's invisible kingdom—and we are the poorer for it.

Have I, myself, ever had an encounter with an angel? Yes, I have. Absolutely. There is no doubt in my mind. You will perhaps question what I am going to tell you, but that is OK. I can understand your skepticism.

I had a tough year in 1997, and a perfect storm of workaholism and delayed grief brought me to my knees. Our youngest daughter had died four years earlier, and I had stuffed my grief in order to keep our family afloat. We left career missions, not returning to Brazil (more grief) shortly after Alex's death, and I re-entered pastoral ministry in North Carolina.

Launching into a new stateside ministry, helping my family survive the loss of Alexandra, and trying to be all things to all people did me in. It was a gradual process, but it was a life-draining process all the same.

For months, I suffered alone, hiding my pain from even my wife. My depression led to anxiety, and my anxiety deepened my depression. This vicious cycle worsened as the months went by, and I became more anxious about being anxious. Panic attacks were something I never thought I would experience, but I did. As a pastor, I had counseled many people suffering from anxiety and depression, but I had never fully appreciated their pain until I suffered the same. I remember praying, *Lord, forgive my lack of understanding and superficiality in trying to help others who I didn't know were suffering so greatly.*

To make a long story short, my depression lasted about a year. I eventually shared my pain with my wife and church leaders, and

Angels

their unwavering support relieved my anxiety significantly. Not having to keep it hidden made a tremendous difference. I began seeing a counselor. He confessed that he, too, had suffered from depression and anxiety and understood what I was going through. This convinced me that I really was not going to lose my mind—and all the gloom and doom I had rehearsed mentally would never occur.

And then I met the angel. I was on my way to an associational meeting in a low mood, still wondering if my life would ever return to normal again. I remember taking the exit off Interstate 40 and only pausing at the yield sign to turn right.

As I turned, out of the corner of my eye, I saw a man holding a sign. I thought, *I did not see that man—or I would have given him some money.* As I drove on, I thought, *I am going back because he might be hungry.*

I turned the car around in a driveway, returned to the exit, and motioned the man over to my window. As he approached, I noticed there was nothing written on his sign. I said, "Sir, I'm sorry. I turned so quickly that I did not see you until it was too late. I wanted to come back to give you this."

As I extended my arm to give him a few dollars, he gently took my arm and pushed it back in the car window. "I do not need your money but thank you. I am here to tell you one thing. You are going to be better. The depression will soon pass. So, do not worry, ok?" As he smiled at me, I could barely mutter the word OK. He patted my arm and went back to where he was standing.

I drove off, stunned, and thought, *what just happened? I can't believe this.* I turned the car around again to go back to talk to the man, but in the two minutes it took me to do so, the man had disappeared—vanished. I will never forget saying out loud in my car, "I just met an angel."

Instead of going on to the meeting, I returned to the church to catch up on some work, still feeling a little shaken by what had just happened. I remember praying something like "Thank you, Lord. Thank you for letting me know that I will be better soon. Thank you for sending me this angel. You are so good. Thank you, thank you, thank you."

Angels

At the end of the day, I headed to my car and, for the first time in months, I heard the birds singing. I smiled and thought, *they are singing for me.* In a matter of days, my depression lifted miraculously—never to return. I still wrestle from time to time with anxiety, but I do not mind. It reminds me that God's grace is sufficient. Like Paul, I bear my thorn gladly.

Did you know that angels were present at practically every important event in the Bible? In fact, angels appear in more than half of the books of the Bible. An angel promised Abraham and Sarah a son—and an angel stopped Abraham from sacrificing that son, Isaac. An angel slew the firstborn sons of Egypt. Angels ministered to the prophet Elijah in the wilderness and protected Shadrach, Meshach, and Abednego in the fiery furnace. An angel kept Daniel unharmed in the lion's den, and it was an angel who told the virgin from Nazareth that she would give birth to the Savior. It was an angel who told the shepherds of Bethlehem that Jesus had been born close by. It was angels that comforted Jesus after his confrontation with Satan in the wilderness as well as after he suffered in prayer in the Garden of Gethsemane. It was angels who proclaimed, "He is risen!" on Easter morning and warned the bewildered disciples not just to stand around idly as Jesus ascended into heaven, but to do what he had commissioned them to do. And lest we forget, scripture teaches that at the Second Coming of Christ, the angels will pour out God's judgment on the earth and accompany our Lord on his return to glory.

Here are four important things scripture tells us about angels:

- God created angels before he created humans (Colossians 1:16). We have no idea how many angels exist, but scripture refers to them as innumerable (Hebrews 12:22). And no, people do not become angels when they die.

- Angels are spirits, but they can temporarily present themselves in forms that can be seen to accomplish God's assigned tasks. Angelic appearances in scripture include as a bright light, fire, and even as ordinary human beings. It seems angels can manifest in limitless ways.

- Angels are extremely powerful beings. They are described in scripture as mighty ones (Psalm 103:20). One angel destroyed the entire Assyrian army as well as Sodom and Gomorrah. As powerful as angels are, only God is omnipotent (all-powerful).
- Angels have great knowledge and wisdom, and they know much more than humans do. However, they are limited in their knowledge because only God is omniscient (all-knowing). We read in scripture that angels rejoice, sing for joy, and worship God with awe and reverence. We might assume since angels have greater intelligence, they are also deeper and more sensitive emotionally.

In Billy Graham's best-selling book, *Angels: God's Secret Agents*, he says, "If you are a believer, expect powerful angels to accompany you in your life experiences. And let those events dramatically illustrate the friendly presence of 'the holy ones' as Daniel calls them."[1]

Dr. Vance Havner once told of an old preacher who worked into the night on a sermon for his small congregation. His wife asked why he spent so much time on a message that he would deliver to so few. He said, "You forget, my dear, how large my audience will be." Nothing is trivial when heaven looks on. Having been a pastor for forty-five years, I have often imagined what looked like empty seats to me filled with heavenly visitors. It gives me added encouragement to do so.

So, do we have guardian angels? This is one of the most asked questions regarding angels, and scripture hints that we do:

> See that you do not despise one of these little ones. For I tell you that their angels in heaven always see the face of my Father in heaven (Matthew 18:10).

The psalmist seems to affirm guardian angels as well:

> For he will command his angels concerning you to guard you in all your ways; they will lift you up in their hands,

---

1. Graham, *Angels: God's Secret Agents*, 37.

Angels

so that you will not strike your foot against a stone (Psalm 91:11–12).

Can angels ever appear as animals? To my knowledge, there is no biblical example that they do. However, if they are spiritual beings taking on what appears to be physical forms at times, could they not appear as a dog if they so desired and God permitted it? If a guardian angel is a person's personal protector and supporter, then a faithful dog could be more than just four feet and a tail. I am thinking of a dog named Diesel. This Old English Bulldog did more for our daughter, Lacey, than any friend ever did. He helped get her through some of the toughest days of her life. She always said that her little sister (Alexandra) sent Diesel from heaven to help fill the void. If Diesel was not an angel, he sure came close—that I know! He certainly was a messenger of love and devotion. You don't have to believe Diesel was an angel if you choose not to. That is OK. However, some beautiful day on the new earth, Lacey, Alex, and Diesel might just jog past your place for the fun of it.

I have always imagined the new earth to be that place where our dreams become more than true. Whatever God loves endures forever in the mind of God. That is why I believe our beloved pets will be there to greet us. A woman once asked Billy Graham if her dog would be in heaven. Billy Graham replied this way:

> God provides us with everything we need to be happy in heaven—and if animals are necessary to make us happy there, you can be confident he will arrange for them to be with us.[2]

Angels are also our mentors when it comes to obedience. Jesus taught us to pray, "Your will be done on earth as it is in heaven" (Matthew 6:10). In heaven, God's will is done perfectly by angels, and their utmost desire is to be God's humble servants. In *Angels: True Stories*, my good friend Robert J. Morgan reminds us that angels are fellow servants with us:

---

2. Graham, "Angels," Syndicated Columnist.

Angels

> In eternity—on the New Earth and the New Heavens and in the celestial city of Jerusalem—We'll be fellow workers and next-door neighbors with angels. We'll be serving the same cause and worshipping the same triune God.[3]

Some have been tempted to worship angels, but this is strictly forbidden in scripture because angels are created beings and servants, as are we. Twice, in the book of Revelation, John the apostle is tempted to fall down and worship the angel, but he is rebuked both times:

> At this I fell at his feet to worship him. But he said to me, "Don't do that! I am a fellow servant with you and with your brothers and sisters who hold to Jesus' testimony. Worship God!" (Revelation 19:10).

> I, John, am the one who heard and saw these things. And when I had heard and seen them, I fell down to worship at the feet of the angel who had been showing them to me. But he said to me, "Don't do that! I am a fellow servant with you and with your fellow prophets and with all who keep the words of this scroll. Worship God!" (Revelation 22:8–9).

Paul also had a warning for the Colossians:

> Do not let anyone who delights in false humility and the worship of angels disqualify you. Such people also go into great detail about what they have seen . . . They have lost connection with the head . . . (Colossians 2:18–19).

What about angels in our dreams? In the first chapter of Matthew's Gospel, we read of Joseph who was engaged to Mary. We know little about him. In the Bible, he never speaks a word, but in a dream, an angel speaks to him:

> Joseph, son of David, do not be afraid to take Mary home as your wife, because what is conceived in her is from the Holy Spirit. She will give birth to a son, and you are to

---

3. Morgan, *Angels: True Stories*, 55.

Angels

give him the name Jesus, because he will save his people from their sins (Matthew 1:20–21).

Some dreams are more important than others. Joseph had dreamed for some time of taking his beloved Mary to be his wedded wife. He looked forward to starting a family and settling down as a skilled carpenter. That dream evaporated when he discovered Mary was pregnant by someone else.

No doubt, Mary had committed adultery. How else could she explain her pregnancy? Being a righteous man, Joseph had no desire to humiliate the woman he loved. He would divorce her secretly and move on with his life. His dream had died until an angel came to him and offered an alternative dream, a better dream, a dream beyond his wildest imagination. This dream helped him understand he was part of a much bigger story.

So, let me ask you again: Do you believe in angels? If yes, have you ever met one (even in your dreams)? I wager you have—whether you recognized it or not. Otherwise, scripture would not warn us to be on the lookout:

> Do not forget to show hospitality to strangers, for by so doing some people have shown hospitality to angels without knowing it (Hebrews 13:2).

We will miss them if we are not careful because they are masterful with their disguises. They are humble, and most of the time, they are anonymous. Do not worry though if you think you've missed seeing angels in this world because you will not miss seeing them in the next.

16

Forgiveness

When Joseph's brothers saw that their father was dead, they said, "What if Joseph holds a grudge against us and pays us back for all the wrongs we did to him?" So they sent word to Joseph, saying, "Your father left these instructions before he died: 'This is what you are to say to Joseph: I ask you to forgive your brothers the sins and the wrongs they committed in treating you so badly.' Now please forgive the sins of the servants of the God of your father." When their message came to him, Joseph wept. His brothers then came and threw themselves down before him. "We are your slaves," they said. But Joseph said to them, "Don't be afraid. Am I in the place of God? You intended to harm me, but God intended it for good to accomplish what is now being done, the saving of many lives. So then, don't be afraid. I will provide for you and your children." And he reassured them and spoke kindly to them.

—Genesis 50:15–21

Forgiveness

If you have ever seen a country church with a bell in the steeple, you will remember that to get the bell ringing you have to tug awhile. Once it has begun to ring, you merely maintain the momentum. As long as you keep pulling, the bell keeps ringing. Forgiveness is letting go of the rope. It is just that simple. But when you do so, the bell keeps ringing. Momentum is still at work. However, if you keep your hands off the rope, the bell will begin to slow and eventually stop.

—CORRIE TEN BOOM

RECENTLY HEARING KAREN CARPENTER sing *Merry Christmas, Darling*, I was reminded of something I heard someone say years ago that I want you to remember, not just as you read these words, but for the rest of your life: *The way we choose to relate to what has happened to us exerts a powerful influence on how we handle what we have not yet experienced.*

The Carpenters, Karen and Richard, dominated the charts in the early seventies, winning several Grammys and even an Oscar. But behind the bright lights of popularity, a dark enemy stalked their success. Karen was starving herself, suffering with an eating disorder, anorexia nervosa.

Her illness can be traced to a music reviewer who referred to her as "Richard's chubby little sister." The reviewer had no idea that from the time Karen was a little girl, she had battled self-esteem and weight problems. Even though she became a music superstar, Karen could not shake the pain of her past—and she died at the age of thirty-two.

Like Karen Carpenter, we all have a past, a past we cannot escape or forget. As William Faulkner famously said, "The past is never dead. It's not even past." That is why the way we relate to what has happened to us is so important. It has lifelong consequences.

Looking back over my life, the person who caused me the most pain was my stepfather. He is probably the only person I have ever really hated, loathed, and despised. As a child, I often prayed that he would die. Later, when my precious mother was dying from cancer at the age of forty, he was having an affair with another woman, which only added to my mother's pain, I am sure. I daydreamed about him dying of cancer someday as a rightful recompence. Sadly, he did, but years later at the age of sixty-six.

I am happy to say that my feelings about my stepfather were upended in the space of one day. It was a miracle really. It was another act of God's providential grace. I was at a conference when a speaker began his presentation this way: "My first name is Theodore. Does anyone know what Theodore means?"

I thought, *yes, it means devil from hell*. Theodore was my stepfather's name. What the speaker said next launched me on a path of healing that I had never dreamed possible.

He said, "Theodore means gift of God."

It was then that I felt the smile of the Holy Spirit in my soul. I knew something would change from that day forward.

I prayed for weeks about what I had heard and felt that day. I began thinking about my stepfather in new ways. There was so much about him that I never knew and never cared to know. When you hate someone as much as I hated him, you only see the bad. But no one person is 100 percent bad. I began trying to remember any good times we spent together in those fifteen years that he was a part of my life. Little by little, the Holy Spirit brought to mind days when things were good between us, and I thanked God for helping me recover those memories. I also thank God for teaching me that hurt people hurt people.

How was my stepfather God's gift to me all those painful years? Looking back now, I see that God was shaping me in ways I could not understand. In my pain, I learned coping skills and survival skills that helped form me as a person and future pastor. I understood the suffering of others on a deeper level, having suffered myself. Growing up in a dysfunctional family equipped me to help others who grew up in similar situations. As Paul beautifully reminds us in 2 Corinthians 1:3–4:

Forgiveness

> Praise be to the God and Father of our Lord Jesus Christ, the Father of compassion and the God of all comfort, who comforts us in all our troubles, so that we can comfort those in any trouble with the comfort we ourselves receive from God.

As I am entering the final stretch of my life, knowing, like Paul, "that my departure is soon at hand," I can honestly say, when I cross the border from this life to the next, that I hope my stepfather is there to greet me, along with everyone else I love. God, in my prayerful imagination, has introduced me to the man I never truly knew but only hated. I look forward to that beautiful place when neither of us is impeded by the consequences of our sins.

What God has helped me do is remember differently. Not forget. Remember differently. Think of that word remember. Re-member, re-frame, re-assemble. We can never completely forget the pain others have caused us, but we can remember it, reframe it, reassemble it with God's help. We can never change the facts, but we can alter how we view them and how we interpret them.

As he was about to retire, Edwin Markham, a poet, discovered that the man to whom he had entrusted his financial portfolio had squandered all the money. Markham's dream of a comfortable retirement vanished overnight.

For a while, he gave in to anger, but one day, while sitting at a table, Markham found himself drawing circles as he tried to soothe the storm within. Love finally had its way, and he thought, *I must forgive him, and I will forgive him.*

Looking again at the circles he had been drawing, he wrote these words:

> He drew a circle to shut me out,
> Heretic, rebel, a thing to flout;
> But love and I had the wit to win,
> We drew a circle and took him in.

Like Edwin Markham, we must learn to transcend the hurt and get to a place in our hearts and minds where the hurt is no longer holding us back from giving ourselves and our gifts fully to

Forgiveness

others. I learned this early from my favorite Bible character, Joseph, son of Jacob. I am relearning it over and over as the years go by.

There are three lessons we can lift from the story of Joseph and how he forgave his brothers:

- Forgiveness is a process and not just a one-time event.
- Forgiveness of very deep hurt takes a long time.
- We need to be patient with ourselves as the healing gradually comes.

C. S. Lewis was badly brutalized by one of his teachers when he was a very young student. This sadistic teacher abused his students by whipping and tormenting them. Eventually, he was declared insane and put away.

Lewis, after becoming a Christian, tried to forgive this teacher. In prayer, he said the words—and he meant it in his heart—but he just could not forget it. Shortly before Lewis died in 1963, he wrote a letter to an American friend:

> Do you know only a few weeks ago I realized suddenly that I had at last forgiven the cruel schoolmaster who so darkened my childhood.[1]

Forgiveness is a process that often takes a long time—so be patient and keep working at it.

In *Tramp for the Lord*, Corrie ten Boom tells the story of how she came face-to-face with one of the cruelest guards at the Ravensbruck Concentration Camp. It was 1947, only three years after the former guard participated in the brutalities that, among other things, took her sister Betsie's life:

> The place was Ravensbruck and the man who was making his way forward was a guard—one of the cruelest guards. Now he was in front of me, hand thrust out: "A fine message Fraulein. How good it is to know that, as you say, all our sins are at the bottom of the sea!"
> And I, who had spoken so glibly of forgiveness, fumbled in my pocketbook rather than take that hand.

---

1. Hooper, C. S. Lewis, *Collected Letters*, Vol.3, 1438.

Forgiveness

> He would not remember me, of course—how could he remember one prisoner among thousands of women?
>
> But I remembered him and the leather crop swinging from his belt. I was face to face with one of my captors and my blood seemed to freeze . . . It could have been many seconds that he stood there—hand held out—but to me it seemed hours as I wrestled with the most difficult thing I had ever had to do.
>
> And still I stood there with the coldness clutching my heart. "Jesus, help me!" I prayed silently. "I can lift my hand. I can do that much. You supply the feeling."
>
> And so woodenly, mechanically, I thrust my hand into the one stretched out to me. As I did, an incredible thing took place. The current started in my shoulder, raced down my arm, and sprang into our joined hands. And then this healing warmth seemed to flood my whole being, bringing tears to my eyes. "I forgive you, brother!" I cried. "With all my heart." I had never known God's love so intensely as I did then. But even so, I realized it was not my love. I had tried, and I did not have the power.[2]

The grace that saves us is the very same grace that will empower us to forgive what seems unforgivable. If grace is not working through us to forgive others, then apparently it has not worked in us to bring about our own forgiveness. That is why Jesus says, "If you cannot forgive, then apparently you have not been forgiven" (Matthew 6:14–15). If you have not experienced grace, you cannot offer it. But if you have experienced grace, you cannot hold it. It must be released, shared.

A second lesson Joseph's story teaches us is that forgiveness is not dependent upon confession or an agreed-upon version of the past. This is very important for us to understand. Joseph forgave his brothers despite their selfish and immature attempt at repenting. We sometimes look at forgiveness as a reward for sufficient groveling and heartfelt apologies, but biblical forgiveness is something God requires of us—and it is not dependent upon the behavior or response of the one being forgiven.

---

2. Ten Boom, *Tramp for the Lord*, 54–55.

Forgiveness

Think of the person who has harmed us and is now dead. I think of my own stepfather. Confession on his part is not possible, but forgiveness on my part is. Joseph knew his brothers were not coming clean, but he forgave them anyway. He did not dig up the past to force them to confess what they had done to him. He didn't say, "Now before I forgive you, I want something to be perfectly clear. Let us get the facts straight on what happened all those years ago." No, Joseph chose to draw a curtain of forgiveness over the past. We must too. Mark Twain was right when he said, "Forgiveness is the fragrance the violet gives to the heel that has crushed it."

Everything was quite good in Bud Welch's life until an April morning in 1995. On that morning, his twenty-three-year-old daughter, Julie, died suddenly and tragically along with another 167 innocent men, women, and children in the bombing of the Murrah Federal Building in Oklahoma City.

Bud Welch said, "I didn't even want Tim McVeigh or Terry Nichols to have trials. I just wanted them dead." After Timothy McVeigh was executed in 2001, Welch decided to search out McVeigh's father and ask if they could meet sometime. I can imagine that McVeigh's father was reluctant at first, but he agreed to the meeting and even invited Bud to visit him in his home.

During the visit, Bud Welch was walking around the elder McVeigh's living room and saw a high school graduation photo of Timothy McVeigh on the mantel. Before even thinking, Welch said, "He was such a good-looking kid."

At that, Timothy McVeigh's father began to sob uncontrollably.

Bud Welch, a conduit for God's forgiveness and grace, understood what was happening. These two fathers had a connection beyond words. They had both lost their children. Bud Welch would later say this was the one event that moved him toward forgiveness and healing more than any other event. In his attempt at closure, God's power fell—and healing began. Pain, shared in faith, manifests peace beyond comprehension.

A third lesson Joseph's story teaches us is that forgiveness is letting go of revenge and turning the person's actions over to God. Joseph refused to retaliate although he had every reason to do so.

Forgiveness

He, however, believed in the providence of God and that human beings are not responsible for the moral balance of the universe. That is God's prerogative alone. "Don't insist on getting even; that's not for you to do. "I'll do the judging," says God. "I'll take care of it" (Romans 12:19, *The Message*). Trusting God's providence did not mean that Joseph's brothers were not responsible for their evil actions. They indeed were. They meant to harm their brother, but God's providential plan overruled their wicked scheme.

I have lived to see God overrule the sin of my stepfather against me—and not just my stepfather, but the sins of others as well. What some meant for harm only moved me closer to God's goal for my life. Once again, the way we choose to relate to what has happened to us exerts a powerful influence on how we handle what has not yet been experienced.

Forgiveness requires that we see on a much deeper level— that we see the humanity of the one who has offended us—and remember that we too possess our own humanity and brokenness. I recall hearing a story about Caroline Kennedy during the time Bill Clinton was being impeached. Her young son saw a picture of President Clinton in the newspaper and said to his mother, "That man is a liar." Seeing it as an important teaching moment, Caroline Kennedy said, "Son, none of us want to be remembered for the worst things we've done. We are more than our worst actions."

And so are we. And so are others—even those you are finding hard to forgive or will find hard to forgive. Since it is impossible to forgive and forget, we must do the next best thing. We must forgive and remember, reframe, and reassemble our memories Godward, allowing God's providence to overrule the offense, the sin, or the evil committed against us. We can never change certain facts, but with God's help, we can alter the way we understand them. Forgiveness never really begins with us anyway. It will always be a response to the One who first forgave us.

Forgiveness

A PRAYER FOR THE POWER TO FORGIVE

Father, please bless me with the power to forgive.
(Bring the person or persons to mind.)
You know the pain they caused, Lord, and I want
to learn to trust you and your providence to
do what I need to do for peace and healing.
Help me let go of all ill will and forgive myself
for my own failings and sin.
Lord, I ask that you not only forgive those
who have hurt me, but also set them free
by the power of your grace.
I know that those who have wronged me
are more than their worst actions. They too
are objects of your unfailing love.
Remind me that that is also true for me.
Thank you for inspiring me, Lord, to
remember, reframe, restructure, and
reassemble what I will never completely
forget so that it will become a blessing
and not a curse.
Through Jesus, our supreme example, who
prayed from the cross, Father, forgive them.
Amen

17

Hope

On the evening of that first day of the week, when the disciples were together, with the doors locked for fear of the Jewish leaders, Jesus came and stood among them and said, "Peace be with you!" After he said this, he showed them his hands and side. The disciples were overjoyed when they saw the Lord. Again Jesus said, "Peace be with you! As the Father has sent me, I am sending you."

—JOHN 20:19–21

The best we can hope for in this life is a knothole peek at the shining realities ahead. Yet a glimpse is enough. It's enough to convince our hearts that whatever sufferings and sorrows currently assail us aren't worthy of comparison to that which waits over the horizon.

—JONI EARECKSON TADA

Hope

WHAT IS YOUR DEFINING story? We all have one, and it matters which story you choose to guide your life. Some kind of narrative shapes the way you view the world and your place in it. Some story is at the core of your identity.

I embraced the story of Jesus decades ago as my defining story, and it has made all the difference in the world. Only God knows the kind of life I would have lived had I chosen some other defining story to make sense of my earthly journey.

I have a friend, Hal West, who was pastor of First Baptist Church, Moncks Corner, South Carolina. Hal and his wife, Elliot, lost their little son, Philip, in 1985. Philip was six years old when he died of leukemia. He battled the disease for about three years.

In the summer of 1984, the year before Philip died, the family dog died, a little cockapoo they had had for twelve years. The children insisted on a funeral, and Hal, my pastor friend, constructed a plywood coffin. They picked out an appropriate spot among some camellia bushes in their backyard to bury their little dog. Philip, age five, his little sister, Laura, age three, and Mom and Dad attended the funeral, and Hal offered a brief prayer thanking God for giving them such a special friend. Then something unexpected happened. This is how my friend, Hal West, describes that day:

> I will never forget, as I began to cover up this tiny coffin, Philip took off into the house without saying a word. I finished pushing down the damp soil, and Elliot and I were trying to console a crying daughter and answer that same old question: "But why did she have to die?"
>
> I remember we were sitting on the ground near the grave when Philip darted out of the house, ran by the three of us, and timidly threw an object in our direction. When I picked it up, I couldn't believe it. I nearly burst into tears myself. Philip had secretly and compassionately constructed a cross of two sticks he had found and bound them together with some scrap pieces of yarn. We called him back and praised him for caring enough to take the time to lovingly make a cross to put on top of the little dog's grave.

Hope

> As I have stated, I don't know how much Philip understood about death, and I'm not sure how much he understood about the cross, but I believe he had an idea that the cross was more than simply a sign of death and a grave marker. I want to believe that in making that cross, he was comforted and strengthened, and that for him, some of the pain of losing an object of love was lessened when he saw the cross standing above the grave where lay the body of his friend.[1]

Philip, a five-year-old child, had a defining story that guided his short life. He believed Jesus cared about him and his little dog—and I do too. In fact, I believe our beloved pets will join us on God's new earth as an added grace. Mark Twain, said, "Heaven goes by favour. If it went by merit, you would stay out and your dog would get in."

A year after the little dog's funeral, Hal, Elliot, and Laura stood at the grave of Philip and remembered what Philip had done when they buried their little dog a year earlier. You can imagine how special the memory was, reminding them of the defining story of their lives—that Jesus lives and, because he lives, our good future is guaranteed.

Calvin Miller beautifully described what awaits those who have placed their faith in the definitive story of the risen Christ:

> I once scorned every fearful thought of death,
> When it was but the end of pulse and breath,
> But now my eyes have seen that past the pain
> There is a world that's waiting to be claimed.
> Earthmaker, Holy, let me now depart,
> For living's such a temporary art.
> And dying is but getting dressed for God,
> Our graves are merely doorways cut in sod.[2]

In John's Gospel, fear had the disciples locked behind closed doors (John 20:19). It was fear of the Jewish leaders, but I think they also feared what we all fear at one time or another: meaninglessness.

---

1. Hipps, *When A Child Dies*, 25–26.
2. Miller, *The Divine Symphony*, 139.

Hope

Had these disciples invested their lives in something that was untrue? Had Jesus misled them? Was he a false prophet misrepresenting the God of Israel—the God he dared call Father and taught his disciples to do likewise? Was he the greatest deceiver of all time?

Meaninglessness—that was my earliest and greatest fear—that life has no meaning—that we are just here for a few years—that we suffer and die, passing into nothingness from which we came. Our children and grandchildren and parents and grandparents and friends will all pass away into nothingness never to be thought of again. There is no Big Story, no personal God, no living Savior, no meaning whatsoever to this thing called life.

And into our fear, the fear of the disciples, your fear, and certainly my fear, walks the risen Jesus, speaking the one word we need to hear the most: *peace*. Not certainty, not explanation, not disclosure—*peace*. We have underestimated the power of God's peace. Our Lord told his disciples that no fear can survive its presence:

> Peace I leave with you; my peace I give you. I do not give to you as the world gives. Do not let your hearts be troubled and do not be afraid (John 14:27).

There it is again as plain as the noses on our faces. Matthew Henry explained how the answer to our fears will always be the peace of Jesus:

> When Christ was about to leave the world he made his will. His soul he committed to the Father, his body he bequeathed to Joseph, his clothes fell to the soldiers, his mother he left to the care of John: but what should he leave to his poor disciples, that had left all for him? Silver and gold he had none; but he left them that which was infinitely better, his peace.[3]

The apostle Paul experienced this peace, and in his letter to the Philippians, he said that the peace of Jesus "transcends all understanding" and "will guard your hearts and your minds" (Philippians 4:7).

---

3. DeHaan, *Windows on the Word*, 108.

Hope

But guard against what? The fears that haunt us every day of our lives. For me, the peace of Jesus has guarded me all my life from the fear of meaninglessness. How exactly? I do not know. It just does. It passes understanding. It has displaced worry with deep peace, deeper than I can explain. God tells us plainly, "My thoughts are not your thoughts, neither are your ways my ways" (Isaiah 55:8), yet we constantly rebel against the truth. The beauty of being perplexed or confused is that it allows us to experience God's peace in the midst of paradox, something that is true even though it may contradict belief and experience. The beauty within contradiction is Jesus's deep, deep peace saturating our uncertainty. Without mystery and self-contradiction, our Christian pilgrimage is based on our limited understanding and our hope in life experiences rather than in God himself.

The supernatural peace of Jesus has challenged me to trust him more than I trust my life experiences, especially those experiences that would generate the most fear. Like grace, the peace of Jesus is free, but it is costly. We receive it through suffering. Peace is the relief after intense struggle. Peace is the knitting together of the loose and dangerous strands of our pain. Peace is that inexplicable trust displayed in the life of Horatio Spafford. After he received news that his children had drowned at sea, he penned these words:

> When peace like a river, attendeth my way,
> When sorrows like sea billows roll
> Whatever my lot, thou hast taught me to say
> It is well, it is well with my soul.

Our Lord Jesus did not promise protection from pain and paradox in this life. He did promise, however, supernatural peace and the absolute certainty that we will be raised with him into everlasting life.

It is good for us to ponder and appreciate the many verses describing the power of God's peace to meet all of life's challenges. Here are just a few we should commit to memory:

> Now may the God of peace, who through the blood of
> the eternal covenant brought back from the dead our

Hope

> Lord Jesus, that great Shepherd of the sheep, equip you with everything good for doing his will, and may he work in us what is pleasing to him, through Jesus Christ, to whom be glory for ever and ever. Amen (Hebrews 13:20–21).
>
> The God of peace will soon crush Satan under your feet (Romans 16:20).
>
> You will keep in perfect peace those whose minds are steadfast, because they trust in you (Isaiah 26:3).
>
> Let the peace of Christ rule in your hearts, since as members of one body you were called to peace. And be thankful (Colossians 3:15).

After England colonized India, they were eager for recreation and decided to build a golf course in the city of Calcutta. Upon completing the project, the English were presented with a unique obstacle. Monkeys would drop out of the trees, run across the course, and steal the golf balls. They would play with the balls for a few minutes, toss them here and there, and then just drop them.

The English golfers soon learned they were powerless to control the monkeys, and they made a new rule: play the ball where the monkey drops it. I love this story because if you think about it, playing golf on this course in India is like what we experience in life. Sometimes the monkeys are good to us, and sometimes they are not. A big part of life will be played from the rough. It is a given, but the supernatural peace of Jesus is also a given.

I have always loved the music of Bill and Gloria Gaither. Their uplifting, faith-building music always points to Jesus and his great love for us. Gloria wrote one song that stands out to me in the early days of their marriage when she was expecting their first child. She and Bill were weathering some difficult days since Bill was seriously ill—and their music was being criticized for not being "spiritual enough." Once again, the beauty of being perplexed or confused is that it allows us to experience God's peace in the midst of paradox. Gloria writes:

Hope

> On New Year's Eve, I sat alone in the darkness thinking about this rebellious world and all of our problems—and about our baby yet unborn. Who in their right mind would bring a child into a world like this?
>
> But then something happened. I can't quite explain what happened in that next moment, but suddenly I felt released from it all—an unexplainable peace.
>
> The panic that had begun to build inside was greatly dispelled by a reassuring presence and a soft voice that kept saying, "Don't forget the empty tomb. Don't forget the empty tomb."
>
> Then I knew I could have that baby and face the future with optimism and trust, for I had been reminded that it was worth it because he lives![4]

Out of that experience, Gloria wrote the words to one of the most loved hymns ever:

> Because He lives, I can face tomorrow,
> Because He lives, all fear is gone,
> Because I know He holds the future
> And life is worth the living (just) because He lives.

Is that your hope? Does the peace of Jesus—the peace that passes all understanding—confirm in your heart that you are going to win the game regardless of where the monkey drops the ball?

I have that hope, and so does another guy from North Carolina. Dr. Eben Alexander wrote *Proof of Heaven: A Neurosurgeon's Journey into the Afterlife*, one of the most talked about books of recent times. Dr. Alexander was a successful academic neurosurgeon for twenty-five years, teaching at both Duke University and Harvard Medical School. He was married with two children and was not particularly spiritual or religious. He was, as he puts it, "a lukewarm Episcopalian who didn't believe in God."

That was true until 2008 when, at the age of fifty-four, Dr. Alexander's life, as it was, came to an end. He was suddenly stricken by a rare illness and went into a coma for seven days. Doctors gave

---

4. Cummings, "Because He Lives."

Hope

no hope for recovery. But he did indeed recover and was forever changed. Documenting his experience, he writes:

> We need to accept—at least hypothetically, and for the moment that the brain itself doesn't produce consciousness. That it is, instead, a kind of reducing valve or filter, sifting the larger, nonphysical consciousness that we possess in the nonphysical worlds down into a more limited capacity for the duration of our mortal lives. The physical side of the universe is a speck of dust compared to the invisible and spiritual part. In my past view, spiritual wasn't a word that I would have employed during a scientific discussion.[5]

He continues, and I think this is the most interesting part of his book:

> During my coma, my brain wasn't working improperly—it wasn't working at all. As a practicing neurosurgeon with decades of research and hands-on work in the operating room behind me, I was in a better-than-average position to judge afterward not only the reality but also the implications of what happened to me. Those implications are tremendous beyond description. My experience showed me that the death of the body and brain are not the end of consciousness, that human experience continues beyond the grave. More important, it continues under the gaze of a God who loves and cares about each one of us and about where the universe itself and all the beings within it are ultimately going. The place I went was real.[6]

As impressive as Dr. Alexander's near-death experience (NDE) was, it pales in comparison to the historic death and resurrection of Jesus Christ. When Jesus died on the cross, it was not a near-death experience. A Roman soldier thrust a spear through his side, releasing a final gush of blood and water to confirm that Jesus was truly dead. His lifeless body was placed in an empty tomb, and

---

5. Alexander, *Proof of Heaven*, 9.
6. Alexander, *Proof of Heaven*, 82.

on the third day, to the shock and surprise of his closest followers, God raised him from the dead.

Luke, a first-century physician, conducted exhaustive research and extensive interviews:

> After his suffering, he presented himself to them and gave many convincing proofs that he was alive. He appeared to them over a period of forty days and spoke about the kingdom of God (Acts 1:3).

Every event in history, including Dr. Eben Alexander's NDE in 2008, is measured by that singular life, that defining story, the story of Jesus Christ.

In living through the paradoxes of life, we must be rooted in the reality of the present—but always with an eye toward the future. The Holy Spirit is forever drawing us forward, toward a time and place that is "not yet." Our defining story is the shared story of a future hope.

The southernmost point of Africa has experienced tremendous storms for centuries. For many years, no one ever knew what lay beyond the cape because no ship attempting to round that point had ever returned. Among the people, it was known as the Cape of Storms and for good reason.

But then, in the sixteenth century, a Portuguese explorer, Vasco da Gama, successfully sailed beyond the point of wild and raging storms to discover a great calm sea and the shores of India. Because of Vasco da Gama, the name of the cape was changed from the Cape of Storms to the Cape of Good Hope. Our defining story says that the door of death now opens to somewhere new because of Jesus. That is our hope, and it is a good hope. Let us not allow the burdens and hardships of this life to distract us or discourage us. Let us keep our eyes firmly fixed on our future, on what God has promised at the end of our journey: home itself.

> Through many dangers, toils and snares,
> I have already come;
> 'Tis grace hath brought me safe thus far,
> And grace will lead me home.

Bibliography

Alexander, Eben. *Proof of Heaven: A Neurosurgeon's Journey into the Afterlife*. New York: Simon & Schuster, Inc., 2012.

Assayas, Michka. *Bono in Conversation with Michka Assayas*. New York: The Berkley Group, 2005.

Benner, David G. *Surrender to Love: Discovering the Heart of Christian Spirituality*. Downers Grove, Illinois: InterVarsity, 2003.

Bixby Knolls Christian Church, n.d. Long Beach, California: Facebook Post.

Bolz Weber, Nadia. "Sermon on the Feeding of the 5000" (preached for pastors, musicians and church leaders). Retrieved from www.patheos.com/blogs/nadiabolzwebber/2015/07/sermon-on-the-feeding-of-the-5000-for-pastors-and-church-leaders.

Brown Taylor, Barbara. *Learning to Walk in the Dark*. New York: Harper Collins, 2014.

———. *Leaving Church: A Memoir of Faith*. San Francisco: Harper Collins, 2006.

Buhler, Brian. "The Ultimate Community." Tape No. 146. Retrieved from https://www.preachingtoday.com/sermons/sermons/2010/july/theultimatecommunity.html.

Campolo, Anthony. *The Kingdom of God Is a Party*. Dallas: Word, 1990.

Coffin, William Sloan. *Letters to a Young Doubter*. Louisville, Kentucky: John Knox, 2005.

Cummings, Tony. "Because He Lives: The story behind a worship/Southern gospel classic." Retrieved from www.crossrhythms.co.uk/articles/music/Because-He-Lives-The-Story-Behind-a-Worship-Southern-gospel-classic/59502/pl.

Dark, David. *The Sacredness of Questioning Everything*. Grand Rapids, Michigan: Zondervan, 2009.

DeHaan, Dennis J., ed. *Windows on the Word*. Grand Rapids, Michigan: Radio Bible Class, 1984.

Dostoevsky, Fyodor. *The Brothers Karamazov*. The Constance Garret Translation: A Norton Critical Edition. New York: Norton, 1976.

Bibliography

Eareckson Tada, Joni. *Heaven: Your Real Home . . . From A Higher Perspective.* Grand Rapids, Michigan: Zondervan, 2018.

Graham, Billy. "Angels." (September 21, 2003) Syndicated Columnist.

———. Angels: *God's Secret Agents.* Nashville: W. Group, 1975.

Green, Stanley W. "Canadian Mennonite." In *1001 Illustrations That Connect*, edited by Craig Brian Larson and Phyllis Ten Elshof. Grand Rapids Michigan: Zondervan, 2000.

Gulley, Philip. *Just Shy of Harmony.* New York: Harper Collins, 2002.

Hipps, Richard. S., ed. *When A Child Dies: Stories of Survival and Hope.* Macon, Georgia: Smyth & Helwys, 1996.

Hooper, Walter. ed. *C. S. Lewis, Collected Letters, Narnia, Cambridge, and Joy, 1950–963. Vol. 3.* London: Harper Collins, 2006.

Joubert, Joseph. *A Selection from His Thoughts.* New York: Dodd, Mead, and Company, 1899.

Kuhlman, Edward. *An Overwhelming Interference.* Old Tappan, New Jersey: Fleming H. Revell Company, 1986.

Kushner, Harold. *When Bad Things Happen to Good People.* New York: Anchor Books, 1981.

Lewis, C. S. *God in the Dock.* Grand Rapids: Wm. B. Eerdmans, 1970.

———. *The Great Divorce.* New York: HarperOne, 1946.

———. *Mere Christianity.* San Francisco: Harper, 1952.

Lloyd-Jones, Sally. *The Jesus Storybook Bible.* Grand Rapids, Michigan: Zondervan, 2007.

Manning, Brennan. *The Ragamuffin Gospel.* Colorado Springs, Colorado: Multnomah, 1990.

McCasland, David. *Oswald Chambers: Abandoned to God.* Grand Rapids, Michigan: Discovery House, 1993.

Merton, Thomas. *Raids on the Unspeakable.* New York: New Directions, 1966.

Miller, Calvin. *The Divine Symphony.* Minneapolis: Bethany, 2000.

Moody Fitt, Emma. *Day by Day with D. L. Moody*—"Devotional for April 19." Chicago, Illinois: Moody, 1977.

Morgan, Robert J. *Angels: True Stories.* Nashville: Thomas Nelson, Inc., 2011.

Newhall, Barbara Falconer. *Wrestling with God: Stories of Doubt and Faith.* Denver, Colorado: Patheos, 2015.

Nouwen, Henri. *Letters to Marc about Jesus.* New York: Harper Collins Publishers, 1987.

Olson, Roger. "Election Is for Everyone." *Christianity Today* (January/February 2013). Retrieved from https://www.christianitytoday.com/ct/2013/january-february/election-is-for-everyone.html.

Peale, Norman Vincent. *The True Joy of Positive Living: An Autobiography.* New York: William Morrow and Company 1984.

Radner, Gilda. *It's Always Something.* New York: Avon Books, 1990.

Rohr, Richard and Mike Morrell. *The Divine Dance: The Trinity and Your Transformation.* New Kensington, Pennsylvania: Whitaker House, 2016.

Bibliography

Sheen, Fulton. J. *Treasure the Clay: The Autobiography of Fulton J. Sheen.* New York: Image Books/Doubleday, 1980.

Shortridge, Stephen. *Deepest Thanks, Deeper Apologies: Reconciling Deeply Held Faith with Honest Doubt.* Brentwood, Tennessee: Worthy, 2011.

Simmons III, Richard E. *The Power of a Humble Life: Quiet Strength in an Age of Arrogance.* Birmingham, Alabama: Union Hill, 2017.

Simon, Art. *Rediscovering the Lord's Prayer.* Minneapolis: Ausburg Books, 2005.

Smedes, Lewis B. *My God and I: A Spiritual Memoir.* Cambridge, UK: William B. Eerdmans, 2003.

Spurgeon, Charles H. *Spurgeon's Sermons,* 9.374, 375, n.d.

———. *The Treasury of the Old Testament, Vol. 3, David's Prayer in the Cave.* Grand Rapids, Michigan: Zondervan, 1951.

Stevens, R. Paul. *Down-to-Earth Spirituality: Encountering God in the Ordinary, Boring Stuff of Life.* Downers Grove, Illinois: InterVarsity, 2003.

Swindoll, Charles R. *Swindoll's Living Insights: Acts: New Testament Commentary.* Carol Stream, Illinois: Tyndale House, 2016.

Taylor, Geraldine Guinness. *Borden of Yale '09.* Philadelphia: China Inland Mission, 1926.

Ten Boom, Corrie. *Tramp for the Lord.* Grand Rapids, Michigan: Fleming H. Revell Company, 1974.

Thomas, W. H. Griffith. *Genesis.* Grand Rapids, Michigan: Eerdman's, 1946.

Tozer, A. W. *The Knowledge of the Holy.* New York: Harper Collins, 1961.

Von Drehle, David, Jay Newton-Small, and Myra Rhodan. "Murder, Race and Mercy, Stories from Charleston." *Time,* November 23, 2015, 43–68.

Willimon, William. *On a Dark and Windy Mountain and 25 Other Meditations for the Christian Year.* Nashville: Abingdon, 1984.

———. *Stories by Willimon.* Nashville: Abingdon, 2020.

Wimber, John. "Signs, Wonders, and Cancer." *Christianity Today* (October 7, 1996) 49–51.

———. "When Do We Get to do the Good Stuff?" Retrieved from http://www.charismatica.com/2009/02/17/john-wimber-when-do-we-get-to-do-the-stuff/.

Yaconelli, Michael. *Dangerous Wonder: The Adventure of Childlike Faith.* Colorado Springs, Colorado: NavPress, 1998.

Yancey, Philip. *What's So Amazing about Grace?* Grand Rapids, Michigan: Zondervan, 1997.

Zahnd, Brian. *A Farewell to Mars.* Colorado Springs, Colorado: David C. Cook, 2014.

www.ingramcontent.com/pod-product-compliance
Lightning Source LLC
Chambersburg PA
CBHW050823160426
43192CB00010B/1869